WRITING ON THE GROUND

By the same author

The Silent Road
A Man Seen Afar
Private Dowding
My Dear Alexia

WRITING ON THE GROUND

BY

WELLESLEY TUDOR POLE

WITH COMMENTARIES BY
WALTER LANG

www.whitecrowbooks.com

Writing on the Ground

First published in 1968.
This edition: Copyright © 2016 by Wellesley Tudor Pole. All rights reserved.

Published and printed in the United States of America and the United Kingdom by White Crow Books; an imprint of White Crow Productions Ltd. in association with Pelegrin Trust and Pilgrim Books.

No part of this book may be reproduced, copied or used in any form or manner whatsoever without written permission, except in the case of brief quotations in reviews and critical articles.

For information, contact White Crow Books
at 3 Hova Villas, Hove. BN3 3DH. United Kingdom,
or e-mail to info@whitecrowbooks.com.

Cover Designed by Butterflyeffect
Interior design by Velin@Perseus-Design.com

Paperback   ISBN 978-1-910121-96-2
eBook   ISBN 978-1-910121-97-9

Non Fiction / Body, Mind & Spirit / Death & Dying

Published by White Crow Books
www.whitecrowbooks.com

Disclaimer: White Crow Productions Ltd. and its directors, employees, distributors, retailers, wholesalers and assignees disclaim any liability or responsibility for the author's statements, words, ideas, criticisms or observations. White Crow Productions Ltd. assumes no responsibility for errors, inaccuracies, or omissions.

CONTENTS

Foreword 7

Introduction 9

Part One

1. Jesus Writes 21
2. "And as Jesus Passed By . . ." 33
3. At Supper 40
4. The Word 62
5. The Problem of Prophecy 74

Part Two

6. Some Links 87
7. The Archangelic Hierarchy 90
8. The Michael Tor, Glastonbury 97
9. The Closing Days of Atlantis 101
10. Does History Repeat Itself? 105
11. Prophecy in Relation to the Day of the Lord . . . 109
12. Chivalry 114
13. Questionnaire 118
14. "And With No Language But a Cry" . . . 129

Part Three

15.	The Baha'i Faith	135
16.	Personal Recollections (Abdu'l Baha Abbas)	140
17.	"Ye are all the Fruits of One Tree"	145
18.	The Fall of Haifa (The Safeguarding of Abdu'l Baha and His Family)	152
19.	The Master as a Seer	156
20.	The Prison House at St. Jean D'Acre (Extract from a letter written in November 1918)	160
21.	Vision on the Mount	166
	Epilogue	168

FOREWORD

Is life extinguished by death or does it continue beyond the grave? The very act of living poses this question and the answer we arrive at—consciously or unconsciously—influences our every thought and every action throughout our lives.

In this book, as in other books by Tudor Pole, this question is neither posed nor answered explicitly. The reason, it seems to me, is that for him the question is irrelevant because the answer to it is an ever present reality, so obvious, so much a part of his life that it is simply taken for granted.

His whole philosophy is a gentle, insistent assertion that the life we know is only a minute part of a greater continuum, existing far back and far ahead.

Tudor Pole's ability to scan this continuum brings glimpses that are denied to most of us. Through this facility or power of access and by the faculties incidental to it, he lifts a curtain on parts of the New Testament story long obscured. The process throws up ideas at once old and new, at once strange and yet familiar: ideas that have a haunting nostalgia suggesting that they are related to something we have always known—perhaps without realising that we knew.

As we read we begin to sense that realities beyond our ordinary horizons are taking shape, and if through T.P.'s writing one can begin to glimpse the outline of the idea behind his words, then one begins to enter with him a dimension where there are no horizons at all and where the very act of entry is found to involve a new kind of experience.

Entry to these new realms is sometimes gentle, sometimes explosive. But whatever the mode of entry, one finds that the view is unexpectedly familiar and that its strange perspectives bring the eternal questions into a new and revealing focus.

I have known T.P. all my life and over the past twenty years or more have been privileged to exchange with him an almost daily correspondence in continuation of my father's more than thirty years of similar interchange with him. Perhaps because of this I have an advantage: some of the new horizons are already half familiar.

Of two things I am completely certain. One is that what he presents is given in absolute sincerity. The other is that if his writing opens up these far horizons for you as it has done for me, your efforts in studying what he says will be amply rewarded.

D. F. O. RUSSELL

INTRODUCTION

Before reading a book like this it is essential to know something about how it came to be written and about the man who is responsible for writing it.

Wellesley Tudor Pole is an elderly man of affairs now living in semi-retirement. He is, however, still active in many fields, keenly interested in the international scene and in the welfare of his fellows.

This is the impression he makes on his neighbours, but it is by no means the whole picture. Among his activities, he is Chairman of the Big Ben Council, London, and of the Chalice Well Trust, Glastonbury. He is also engaged in correspondence with various sections of the Press overseas and with societies working for brotherhood and understanding between all nations; and he still retains a number of industrial interests.

To his many associates in commerce he is a thoroughly practical business man with a specialised knowledge of the Near and Middle East. There appears to be nothing unusual about him.

They would therefore probably be startled to discover that he has quite a different side to his life. This might be called his invisible reputation, and it is very far indeed from being ordinary.

Many people—and they are scattered all over the world—believe that he is a seer, an example of a rare type of individual well known in pre-Classical times; recognised

INTRODUCTION

and accepted as a phenomenon in the Middle Ages; but strangely without place or even adequate description in the modern world.

The idea of the man who sees differently from other men is best placed in a context which is well known in certain circles but is surprisingly unfamiliar elsewhere.

The idea, in its essentials, is that certain expanded levels of consciousness, certain modes of cognition beyond the ordinary are included as possibilities in every human being. But in almost all of us they are only potential—like a baby's ability to ride a bicycle.

Sometimes such possibilities become actual in certain individuals; and the life of such a man foreshadows a situation which, for the commonality, lies far ahead in the evolution of the race.

Is this a fantastic idea? It has some support at physical level. The biologist looks at the record of evolution and sees, time and time again, the emergence of some creature endowed with wholly novel physical structure, apparently useless and sometimes even preposterous in terms of its place and time. Yet these novelties—the hint of a backbone the first tentative prototype of a nervous system, the first opposable thumb—can be seen in hindsight as feeble gropings towards an unimaginable future.

T.P. makes no claims of any kind and he firmly discourages those who make them for him. Indeed, he discourages all personal inquiry. At the same time, such claims are implicit in all his writing and it is dishonesty to attend to the one and pretend you haven't noticed the other.

The clear conclusion for those who know him well—and for many who have merely studied his writing—is that Tudor Pole is able to live in two worlds and to pass information about another world (to a limited and cautious extent) to people in this.

To avoid compromise with the terminology of science, mysticism and religion, he refers to everything beyond the register of the ordinary senses as the *au-delà*. Now this dual passport, if it exists, should not be evaluated in terms of spiritualistic trance or religious ecstasy. It is nothing like that. It appears to be—and this is where it is so very rare—the development of a faculty of mind which is able to by-pass the infra-world of psychism and another area where an interim reward of "beauty" and "ecstasy" may be mistaken for the final goal.

Whatever the faculty, it goes through, in simple consciousness, to an *au-delà* where there is unity instead of diversity, method instead of madness, order instead of chaos; and where some unimaginable order of things proceeds on a single fiat; love.

For many years T.P. has been distributing spiritual gold, generally by stealth. Sometimes glimpses of higher laws are given to a correspondent (he has hundreds who have never met him), in the context of some advice on a personal problem.

Often, higher insights are wrapped in an amusing traveller's tale. Sometimes, as in his book *The Silent Road* a great vista of cosmic purpose is skilfully embedded just below the surface of some charming but trivial vignette.

An outstanding example of his external activities was the Silent Minute campaign. As with so many of T.P.'s interests there was in this a strange quality suggesting that he was in some way reconciling past and future through an action in the present.

INTRODUCTION

The idea began in 1917 when two British officers were discussing the war and its probable aftermath.

The conversation took place in a billet on the hillside at the mouth of a cave in the Palestine hills, and on the eve of a battle. One of the two, a man of unusual character and vision, realising intuitively that his days on earth were to be shortened, told his friend, who was Tudor Pole: "I shan't come through this struggle and, like millions of others, it will be my destiny to go on. You will survive and live to see a greater and more vital conflict fought out in every continent and ocean and in the air. When that times comes, remember us. We shall long to play our part. Give us the opportunity to do so, for that war will be a righteous war. We shall not then fight with material weapons, but we will be able to help you if you will let us. We shall be an unseen but mighty army. You will still have 'time' as your servant. *Lend us a moment of it* each day and through your silence give us our opportunity. The power of silence is greater than you know. When those tragic days arrive do not forget us."

Next day the speaker was killed. W.T.P. was severely wounded and left with the enemy, but managed to get back to the British lines, with an inescapable sense of miraculous deliverance.

The idea of the Silent Minute was thus born in Palestine in December 1917. It came to external realisation in the dark days of Dunkirk twenty-three years later when Britain stood alone and unprotected against overwhelming forces of evil. Men and women of goodwill in England and throughout the Commonwealth and elsewhere were then asked to devote one minute of their time at nine each evening to a prayer for peace, and thus to create a channel between the visible and the invisible worlds. The movement grew until unknown numbers were united in keeping this evening tryst. This dedicated Minute received the warm support of H.M. king George VI, Mr. Winston Churchill, his Cabinet and many other leaders in Church and State. The value was fully realised by the late President Roosevelt and by our Allies from overseas. The Minute was observed on land, air and sea, on the battlefields, in air-raid shelters, hospitals and prison camps, and in the homes of poor and rich alike.

At T.P.'s request and with the Prime Minister's support, the B.B.C. restored the voice of Big Ben to the air on Remembrance Sunday, November 10th, 1940, as a signal for the Silent Minute at nine each evening; and this became accepted practice in the Home and Overseas Service for the remainder of the war years and for some time afterwards.

According to the B.B.C. the number of those observing it in Britain and Europe from 1942 onwards ran into many millions.

Soon after the end of hostilities in Europe in 1945 a British Intelligence officer, interrogating high Nazi officials, asked one of them why he thought Germany had lost the war. This was the reply:

"During the war you had a secret weapon for which we could find no counter-measure and which we did not understand, but it was very powerful. It was associated with the striking of Big Ben each evening. I believe you called it "the Silent Minute."

Clearly the significance of the Silent Minute must be assessed from a viewpoint far removed from ordinary standards of judgement.

INTRODUCTION

A second example of T.P.'s venture is Chalice Well, in Glastonbury.

In 1904 he first saw the site of Chalice Well. It lies at the foot of Glastonbury Tor, just off the main road between Glastonbury and West Pennard. It was then part of a property belonging to a Roman Catholic order. He recognised the sanctity of the place and saw much else concerning it. He felt that a future purpose depended on this site for its manifestation and he resolved to make every effort to acquire it so soon as an opportunity occurred.

He declared this intention to Cardinal Gasquet, who at that time was Abbot President of the English Benedictine Order, when he stayed with him at Tor House in 1907.

In 1909, following the sale of the Glastonbury Abbey ruins to the Church of England, the Chalice Well site passed into private hands. Half a century later, T.P.'s aim was finally realised. The property came on the market and he was able to arrange for its purchase.

Since then the place has become a focal point for pilgrims from all over the world. There are no relics, no rituals. The place simply inheres a purpose. There are orchards and a garden, there is a spring of water and there is an atmosphere. People sense it and feel no need for explanation.

Was it in this area that the first Christian church in the world was built? Did Joseph of Arimathea come here after the crucifixion? And if so, who came with him? Why should the Grail legend focus so enduringly in this district? And if it is all legend, all mumbo-jumbo, is it not strange that in the conclaves of Rome before memory was ousted by political pressure, precedence was given at

INTRODUCTION

Roman and other Christian councils to the delegate from Britain before all others?

Chalice Well itself derives from a spring of underground water and is sited in an inspiring, flower-filled garden. To normal vision it seems unimportant. But by what standards do we judge importance? How many can see what might be called noumenal meaning? Not many saw much happening in A.D. 33.

Could it be that at the present time—particularly at the present time—there is a shifting of the moves which we glimpse here below as trivial and disconnected, but which from a higher viewpoint form part of a grander whole, both coherent and imperative.

In 1965 in collaboration with his friend Rosamond Lehmann he produced a book which is now a treasured possession for many of us—*A Man Seen Afar*.*

The material for this, though prepared for during many years of mind training and discipline, was received, as he says, "spontaneously and naturally" over a period of less than three months.

It amounts to a delineation of a small historical area of space and time concerned with Jesus, his daily circumstances and his mission.

It is a picture which in places amplifies and in places contradicts the Gospel accounts. These insights produce, as Rosamond Lehmann said, a kind of shock, as of inner recognition, stilling attention without conscious effort, a "touchstone" quality that made all question of evidence or proof seem to her irrelevant. The "glimpses" do indeed have this quality. Merely reading them produces a subtle

* Published by Neville Spearman.

INTRODUCTION

change in our spiritual outlook. They may do more. They lead to a qualitative change in our understanding.

If they do, is there any background against which such a realignment could be seen as significant?

Is there perhaps some work-target of the epoch which requires that the existing records should be adjusted? My conclusion is that T.P. believes so. Were I to leap into conjecture—but based almost entirely on what I have learnt from T.P.—this is what I would deduce:

We are moving out of one age and into another. Energies beyond the frontiers of human perception are preparing to release into humanity a new impulse. This, if rightly received, will be capable of transforming human life on earth. But the impulse is unlikely to break through unless certain conditions involving human co-operation are made available.

Without this adjustment, work on the Aquarian building site cannot be started, or if started, could only perpetuate an existing distortion in the lower floors of the Piscean building beneath.

It would be simple, one might think, to show this in terms of the sweeping cosmic insights which T.P. appears to possess. Yet he chooses to do it—or is under orders to do it—by certain alterations to our picture of the historical Jesus.

To outer understanding there would seem to be easier, more factual ways of correcting historical errors. For example, there is in existence (and known to Tudor Pole) a record of a certain series of events hitherto unknown to history. Data relevant to these events many centuries ago, exist intact and await archaeological discovery. Yet T.P. dismisses all suggestions that further information should be

INTRODUCTION

disclosed. The time, he says, is not yet. He chooses instead to introduce gradually the correction—and perhaps the erosion—which he believes to be necessary. The method, for him right and lawful, is the publication of these glimpses of the historical Jesus.

My own feeling is that T.P.'s work is part, perhaps a small part, of a world-wide operation at present being mounted by the higher powers.

Probably many people widely dispersed in the world, some known, some unheard of, are engaged in it, each discharging his own fraction of a total mandate.

The work is to rewind the spiritual transformer of the planet in a different way, to prepare for a new flow of current from a solar source. How we do this rewinding at the present time will determine how the current will flow; and the manner of its flowing will determine the resonant frequency of humanity for the coming times.

Few if any of those taking part will see the work in its entirety. Some, perhaps, like T.P. will be fully aware of their own role. Others, willing but less comprehending, will be drawn to play a part they only very dimly perceive.

Round all these centres there will be a periphery of ordinary people compelled by a simple urgency to converge on a building site which they cannot see at all.

So it probably was 2,000 years ago. It may even be that units which worked together then are working together now, meeting familiar fellows and forming nostalgically familiar relationships, sensing it all fleetingly and disjointedly like components of a haunting dream.

About such a concept there is much that is hopelessly illogical. Even the building bricks of the project seem illogical. For example not all of the material given out

INTRODUCTION

recently by T.P. seems concerned at all with the Jesus glimpses which are his main preoccupation. Obliquely he drops in other material which to the outward eye, seems irrelevant. Yet it *has* been injected into the main stream and we can only conjecture that it has a relevance, real and immediate, in some context of which we are unaware.

The belief that all of it inholds some coherence at some level, is, in essence, an act of faith. But faith is evidence of things unseen; and of things unseen in relation to T.P. we have abundant evidence.

Some time ago it became apparent that he proposed to extend the glimpses given in *A Man Seen Afar* and to my alarm insisted that I should collaborate.

I have reservations alike about clairvoyance and about mysticism. I have never talked to a departed relative, never had a religious experience. From both the orthodox and the heterodox aspects of the transcendental, it would be difficult to find anyone more extensively *unqualified* to work with Tudor Pole.

Yet he insists that I should introduce these new glimpses, edit them, collate them and comment on them. More, he assumed that it was a foregone conclusion that I would do so.

In agreeing, I made the single condition that I would do it according to my lights (if any) and this, so he says, is precisely what is wanted. I can only assume that this is an example of what Huxley called "grace in queer places".

WALTER LANG

Part One

CHAPTER ONE

Jesus Writes

They said unto him Master, this woman was taken in adultery, in the very act.

Now Moses in the law commanded us that such should be stoned: but what sayest thou:

This they said, tempting him, that they might have to accuse him. But Jesus stooped down and with his finger wrote on the ground, as though he heard them not.

So when they continued asking him he lifted himself up and said unto them, He that is without sin among you, let him first cast a stone at her.

John viii. 4, 5, 6, 7

And again he stooped down, and wrote on the ground.

John viii. 8

W.T.P. The account given in St. John, Chapter viii, of events surrounding the "Writing on the Ground" needs elucidation. The writer of this Gospel condensed his material to such an extent that he gave a very incorrect picture of a series of events which covered a two-day period, a Friday and a Saturday. Verses one to eleven deal with happenings on the Friday. From verse twelve onwards the events recorded took place on the Sabbath. St. John, Chapter ix, refers to incidents that occurred much

JESUS WRITES

later and on quite a different occasion. They should not be read as directly following on from the previous chapter, although repetition of the words "passed by" tend to give this impression.

The narrator of the writing on the ground incident was evidently relying on dubious hearsay "evidence". Certainly Jesus did not stoop down in the Temple, as seems indicated in verse two, and attempt to write on the marble slabs which paved both the Temple itself, its corridors and the adjoining courtyards. He wrote on virgin soil, in the open air. The catapulting of many incidents into a single place and at a particular time can but cause confusion and upset important sequences.

Perhaps it might be useful here if I gave an account of Jesus' movement throughout that momentous Friday. I make no claim to complete accuracy in every detail and am quite prepared to face incredulity.

Jesus and his disciples had reached Jerusalem at a period when the city was already crowded for the approaching Passover season. Unrest was in the air. Jesus went to the town house of Joseph of Arimathea, with whom he had often stayed, and fortunately found his uncle at home. The latter was a kindly but forceful man, one who rarely minced his words. He told Jesus that it would be dangerous for him to be seen in and around the city, in company with his immediate followers. He warned Jesus that the police, both religious and secular, were on the alert and that the movements of such a large group would attract hostile attention and possible arrest.

At the time the disciples' communal purse was almost empty and whilst the Master willingly accepted his uncle's hospitality for himself, he refused to burden him with the additional expense of housing and feeding more than two of his disciples at a time. This was one of several occasions when the unseen powers of negation tried to separate Jesus from his disciples and to break up this small community once and for all. In fact, the only occasion when they scored a temporary success took place at the time of Jesus' arrest in the Garden, about a year later.

Acting on Joseph's advice, Jesus advised ten of the disciples to go their ways for the time being. Those who had been fishermen returned to see their families in Galilee and to earn a little money by fishing. Several of the others left for Judea to work on the farms and estates belonging to Joseph, as a temporary means of earning their livelihood. Judas left for Beersheeba, to arrange the sale of a plot of land which he had recently inherited from his father. Altogether it was not a happy time for those concerned and the future seemed to hold little but obscurity and doubt.

Early on the Friday morning Jesus left Joseph's home and went alone to the Mount of Olives. He realised the importance of the day and needed to prepare for it in prayer, meditation and silence. Later that morning when the sun was up, he retraced his footsteps and went into the Temple and spoke at length to the thronging crowd. At this point the sequence of events is recorded incorrectly in the Gospel narratives. Towards midday Jesus left the Temple and mingled with the crowd buying wares in one of the courtyards.

At a stall there he was offered a gourd of goat's milk which he accepted gratefully, this being the only food he had consumed that day. In the early afternoon the Master, wishing to be alone, shook off the crowd and found his way into an open garden "court" and there he sat down under a cedar tree and fell asleep for a while.

Here is an impression of the scene as viewed by an onlooker an hour before the great event of the Writing on the Ground. The season was spring, mid afternoon on a warm mellow sunlit day. Unless calculation errs, these happenings took place in the April of our modern calendar and at the beginning of the third year of Jesus' public Ministry. It would be misleading to describe the place as if it were a formal Temple courtyard and in any case it was situated beyond the Temple's immediate environs, being separated from them by the paved and partly covered courts which surrounded the Temple's precincts. These courts were nearly always crowded, and several of them contained market stalls similar in appearance to the oriental bazaars to be seen in any Arab town today. Fruit, vegetables and general merchandise were on sale there for six days each week. The archways beneath the outer corridors to the Temple itself were reserved for the use of the "elite", namely the money changers and usurers who paid heavy dues to the High Priest for their privileged position. The sale of doves took place in the open air and in the area between the Temple steps and these paved and walled courtyards where the general traffickers plied their wares.

The place which I have described as a "courtyard" was situated near the outer perimeter of the Temple property and was in fact no more than a rustic garden, very much in fallow, low walled, its surface being natural ground, sandy and without paving stones or similar adornments. Beneath a wild pear tree in a corner of this "garden" could be seen the wooden superstructure of a well. The spring which fed it must have lain deep below the ground, because the pulleys of the well showed signs of being worked by a donkey winch. In the shade of a nearby olive tree stood a donkey, evidently tired by the labours of the day.

Under the shadow of the wall itself were to be seen a row of large earthenware pitchers filled with water. Their mouths were covered by the leaves of a wild vine which climbed all along that section of the wall.

A boy of about fifteen lay on the ground beside the donkey, mounting guard over the pitchers and their precious contents. When evening set in, Temple servants would arrive to take the pitchers to the High Priest for the blessing of the water they contained. This marked the day as being almost certainly a Friday, when, towards midnight, the ceremonial pre-Sabbatical ablutions would take place according to the law.

Near the centre of this wild garden courtyard stood a venerable cedar, and beneath its friendly branches several roughly hewn wooden seats had been rivetted into the ground.

At the time we are reviewing, Jesus sat on one of these, alone and in deep meditation. How rarely was he able to be alone! And this time not for long. Soon the noise of distant tumult disturbed his peace. It was the duty of the Temple guard on Fridays before dusk to round up and disperse the beggars and mendicants who thronged the sacred precincts throughout the week, but who were not allowed this access during the Sabbath. A group of these unfortunates found their way into the garden courtyard where Jesus sat. He called them over to him and signalled to the donkey boy to bring fresh water from the well. This he shared with them whilst they knelt on the ground around him. What passed between them is unrecorded, but its effect was evident in the joy on their faces as they rose to go their ways out into the countryside stretching beyond this garden in the direction of Mount Scopus. (The Vale and Garden of Gethsemane lay well away to the south-west, and beyond view.)

Soon afterwards a group of Pharisees with, in their midst, a woman, dragged reluctantly along, came hurrying into this garden place, in search of Jesus. I believe her name was Miriam. She was a comely woman of the people, not a member of the "unfortunate class" but happily married to a foreman baker of the city, her one lapse into unfaithfulness giving the Pharisees just the opportunity they sought.

"They said unto him, Master, this woman was taken in adultery in the very act. Now Moses in the law commanded us that such should be stoned; but what sayest thou?"

Unexpectedly to those around him, the Master fell silent for a while. Then he stooped down and wrote with his finger upon the ground. Then he rose up and gave the Pharisees their answer. Once more he stooped down, and, using his finger as a sword, wrote upon the ground for a second time.

After the Pharisees and the small crowd around them had melted away, Jesus called to the donkey boy and told him to escort the woman to her home. Meanwhile he promised to look after the donkey and to feed and water him.

And so at dusk, the High Priests' servants, arriving to transport the water-jars to the Temple, were amazed to see a solitary figure talking to a donkey as if to a familiar friend.

JESUS WRITES

About this time Joseph has become alarmed at the Master's long all-day absence and sent two of his servants to look for him. Darkness fell before they found him, and meanwhile the boy had returned; and after thanking and blessing him, Jesus allowed himself to be escorted back to Joseph's home.

This is as clear a picture as I can give of the happenings on that momentous Friday; and my own view is that this picture is more accurate in sequence and in detail than that which is set forth in Gospel narratives.

From the viewpoint of a lowly onlooker this was all that happened. There was an "incident" in an open air courtyard adjoining the Temple in Jerusalem; Jesus wrote with his finger in the dust; some Pharisees were discomfited; and a woman was saved from a brutal death.

A seer watching the same scene from a higher dimension would have seen something quite different. He would have seen a stupendous, a cosmic act.

In my view Jesus was the instrument for fulfilling a special act at a particular moment of "Time" which had not been attempted in this Round by any of his predecessors. There is a basic and master rhythm which controls and infuses planetary life energies of every kind and form. One could describe it as creating a central vibratory keynote which vitalises and sustains the continued existence of the primary atom; from which atom planetary life, however manifested, is derived and on which it depends for its existence.

Jesus' central task during this three years' Ministry was to act as the medium for "earthing a Cosmic 'current'" (for want of a better description) in such a way as to heighten and quicken the vibratory rate and the rotation of the rhythmic processes governing all planetary activities. Jesus spoke of bringing a sword with him and this sword (of the spirit) was the instrument he used for carrying out the "earthing" process. He also spoke of bringing "Life" with him, that is, a renewal of our planetary life destined to be ushered in by a change of rhythm.

All else was secondary; but the successful achievement of his task produced such an overpowering effect upon him, that he was lifted above time and space and "saw" the Coming of the Kingdom on earth. He saw it, however, as if it were imminent and not a long term result of what he had been allowed to do. The current of which I speak passed through him and then into his sword and so into the very living soil and structure of the planet. Whether he was fully aware of the process "as a man" we do not know, in the same way that it is uncertain whether he always realised the full import of what was said through him by the Christos.

My surmise is that his accomplishment as outlined above was unique in world history in method and operation up to the point at which he appeared among us. What happened would have destroyed his human form, had it not been that this form held in perfect balance and rapport the masculine and feminine qualities and instincts inherent in human nature. In other words, Jesus could act as a perfect lightning conductor, without causing any damage to his mind or body.

"And again he stooped down and wrote on the ground". It was on this second occasion that the impulse passed through him which set in motion the rhythmic changes in planetary life.

JESUS WRITES

No fanfare of trumpets, no sound of thunder, no burning bush marked the consummation of this stupendous act. A seer watching from a higher dimension would have observed the Master, standing erect, head held high, sword grasped in both hands, the shining blade pointing downward to the ground and to the living depths beneath.

Two acts in one? Both of them were of great significance but the second act was of import far beyond our comprehension. The combination of the two holds a meaning which each one of us should work out for himself.

Though the incident of the writing on the ground earthed energies of a cosmic character to the planet, another act by Jesus was necessary to ensure that they would be retained.

Jesus carried out this anchoring process during the time he spent, after his Crucifixion in the Underworld (not Hell). This means literally what it says, namely the underground area of our planet, the depths of the earth. It was here that the quickened Rhythm, which he had already "earthed" was anchored in such a way as to ensure permanency until the next change in the wavelength of the Rhythm should become necessary (an event that is likely to happen before the present century is out).

I think Steiner speaks of the Christ Impulse impregnating the earth during the three days which followed the Crucifixion, but I have never seen the lecture in which he is said to have made this statement. It certainly contains an element of truth.

Lang: The foregoing narrative raises many speculations. Could an event, significant not only for Christians, not only for humanity but for the whole rhythm of the biosphere have gone almost unrecorded and certainly uninterpreted for 2,000 years? If we accept T.P.'s insight there is no escape from the answer. Yes. The truth for T.P. appears to lie in a viewpoint which Christian theology has always been reluctant to inspect; the viewpoint from which the Christ is seen as infallible and omniscient, but Jesus is seen as something at least a little short of a totally perfect instrument.

Here there is a conflict in T.P. On the one hand he is concerned lest anything that follows from his insights should appear to support the slightest denigration of the historical Jesus. His affection for Jesus is profound to a point which most of us can probably hardly imagine.

After sending me one script he followed it with a letter saying:

> I make insufficient allowance for the immense pressures to which Jesus was subjected. Please modify or delete any seeming criticisms of Jesus' apparent shortcomings as viewed from the records available to us.

On the other hand T.P.'s mandate appears to be the correction of certain misconceptions in the historical account. If this involves plain recognition that Jesus, as distinct from the Christ everlighting him, was not infallible, what then?

Sometimes, perhaps daring more than we can know, T.P. is obliged to come out unequivocally with an assertion such as this:

"Jesus as a man had no personal experience of the sexual conflicts which have been humanity's common heritage since the Fall when unity was replaced by duality. Perhaps this lack of experience was the reason why he made no attempt to deal with specifically sexual problems."

The idea of the human fallibility of Jesus runs through much that T.P. has seen and feels obliged to give out. It is a matter to which we shall have to return again, particularly in connection with the relationship of Jesus to the prophetic tradition of Judaism.

Then there is a very "leading" sentence which says, "The narrator of the writing on the ground incident was evidently relying on dubious hearsay evidence."

No tendency here to regard the Gospels as accounts divinely inspired, tailored in their final form and as Shaw said, "delivered from Heaven in a plain van".

There is the clear belief that they were by no means infallible. Indeed in a letter T.P. declares his position beyond any possibility of doubt. "That John of the Supper did not write John's Gospel is in my view a self evident certainty. I don't think any of the four except probably Mark wrote their Gospels although they may have been consulted as and when available."

This does not however rule out the possibility of an "autonomous" gospel. T.P. believes that John ("the only disciple who really understood Jesus' teaching") in his old age dictated to Polycarp his personal account of the life and teaching of Jesus and that this first person account exists to this day and may even be recovered before the close of this century.

It is interesting to note the points in the script where there is a subtle erosion of accepted ideas. For instance "At the time the disciples' communal purse was empty and whilst the Master willingly accepted his uncle's hospitality for himself he refused to burden him with the added expense of housing and feeding more than two of his disciples at a time." Here there is plain recognition of the facts of everyday life, agreement that even men engaged in a spiritual event of the highest magnitude were not absolved from rendering unto Caesar.

There is a welcome quality about this reassurance of simple normality; an implied assertion that Christian living is not necessarily sited in some etherialised region where scrip and purse are unnecessary, but in Jerusalem or Rome or on the M.1 where they manifestly are.

CHAPTER TWO

"And as Jesus Passed By ..."

W.T.P. The impression left on many who read the New Testament accounts of Our Lord's wandering up and down the countryside during his Ministry and for some years previously is distorted and entirely out of perspective.

He is pictured as leading a nomadic existence, restless and always on the move, passing through one village or hamlet after another and never stopping anywhere for long. According to this view Jesus and his immediate followers spent the whole year, winter and summer, in an almost endless series of tramps and pilgrimages, rarely venturing beyond the frontiers of Palestine itself. The impression given is that he and his devoted band lived like mendicants, dependent for sustenance and shelter on the alms and hospitality of village folk and of the common people of the countryside, without a fixed abode, ceaselessly leading a gypsy existence. How can we accept such a concept as representing the facts? The historians who based their Gospel narratives on rumour and hearsay "evidence", even if the disciples themselves may have lent their names to such "recollections", show by the contents of their stories that these do not carry the imprimatur to be expected from actual witnesses of the scenes described. What we find strangely lacking is the almost complete absence of the personal touch.

The writers or inspirers of the Gospels are supposed to

"AND AS JESUS PASSED BY..."

be men who had shared their daily lives with Jesus, day in, day out over a period of several years. How is it that we rarely if ever come across personal reminiscences of such events recorded by these writers, said to have been on the spot? We never read such passages as this: "I remember an occasion when we were staying for a few days in Bethany. One evening our Master asked me to accompany him up the hillside behind the house, in order to share the glories of the sunset with him. He spoke to me about the true sunshine of the heavenly realms, and later he gave me some good advice about a personal problem, then causing me such much anxiety."

Naturally such reminiscences would have been worded in the vernacular of the period but their complete absence must leave us wondering whether the authors or compilers of the Gospels were the same men who had been the intimate and daily companions of Jesus?

I believe that experts differ as to the identity of the "John" who compiled the Gospel of that name. It is difficult to believe that the disciple John, closest confidant of the Master's inner circle, could have written this Gospel. He took a prominent part in the sacrament of the sharing of the bread and the wine, for it was he who handed Jesus first the bread and then the cup. John's Gospel does not think that this momentous and unique event was even worth mentioning in the course of his somewhat casual reference to Supper!

Luke is generally accepted as being the compiler of the "Acts" but these contain nothing about the Last Supper.

Returning to the question as to whether Jesus led a life of vagabondage during most of his mature years, surely

"AND AS JESUS PASSED BY..."

the time has come to end once and for all such distortions of the facts?

The daily life of Jesus and those around him followed a far more normal and natural course than is inferred by the Gospel writers. They certainly travelled a great deal in fulfilling the Mission for which they had been brought together, but they were not continually on the move.

At the southern tip of the Sea of Galilee, in a sheltered fold of the ground what might be described as a home base had been set up early in the period of the three years' Ministry. Good friends of the disciples had created here a kind of homestead. Huts and tents were provided and several caves in the vicinity had been rendered habitable for use in inclement weather. A spring of fresh water nearby bubbled forth into a small stream which ran down into the Lake. This little valley, a small oasis, in fact, contained several fig trees, palms and fruit-bearing bushes. A goatherd and his wife lived further up the valley, acting as caretakers of this modest settlement at all times. At least twice a year, often for a month at a time, the "Jesus Community" would live in this improvised homestead and rest from their labours.

Several of the disciples belonged to these parts and there would be an interchange of visits with their relatives who lived in villages around the lake. When a sudden call for help was received, perhaps on behalf of a sick child or because of the unexpected drying up of a village well, Jesus would either interrupt his rest or send one of the twelve, to bring whatever help was needed. Probably the spring of which I speak is no longer there, or it may have been converted into a stone-lined well, of which many are still extant in that area.

"AND AS JESUS PASSED BY..."

This was not the only resting place available to Jesus and his friends. On one of his Judean properties Joseph of Arimathea had set aside a suitable site not far from one of his farm houses, where hutments had been erected beneath the shade of olives and wild oaks. For Jesus this was a very favourite spot and he spent as much time as he could spare in these healthy and friendly surroundings.

I should not omit reference to another resting place which was very dear to the Master's heart. By good fortune close friends of John owned a small farm oasis about a mile inland from Akka. When pressures became great John would take Jesus to this lovely semi-secluded spot, sometimes for a week or two in retreat and alone.

I hope I have done something to bring a little true perspective into the Gospel stories. We should dismiss from our minds the notion that Our Lord was eternally "passing by", a homeless, wandering Jew, scorned, rejected and an outcast from the natural life of the country in which he lived and taught. Enemies there were, especially among the orthodox and wealthy. They reacted violently not so much against Jesus' general outlook on life as to his exhortations to the rich to share their bounty with the sick and poor.

However, it is wrong to believe that active persecution continually interfered with our Lord's Ministry or upset the serenity of his daily life. It was only during the last few months of his sojourn among us that he and his followers were subject to serious molestation and police supervision.

It was during this period that much of what he said in public appeared to the Jewish and Roman authorities to

"AND AS JESUS PASSED BY..."

contain political implications of a kind likely to disrupt public order and security.

Up to this time Jesus had enjoyed his life and to picture him as a "Man of Sorrows" is very wide of the mark. Naturally times of depression were not entirely absent over the years, and even occasional periods of doubt and frustration, but he was normally happy, a man of joy, immensely cheered by the devoted love of the common people and buoyed up by the ever-living presence of the Christ spirit within himself. Above all his vision reached heights from which could be clearly perceived the ultimate triumph of his Father's plans for the Universe and all creation.

Lang: Again the outstanding feature of this narrative is its down-to-earth quality, the extent to which it fixed the mission of Jesus firmly in the everyday world of ordinary men.

But here, also, perhaps for the first time ever, there is a hint of the practical planning that must have accompanied the mission. One can almost catch snatches of conversation between them. "Would it not be better if we waited here till. . . .?" "If we went to Joseph's place now we could . . ." and Jesus either nodding agreement or shaking his head in veto, responding not to expediency but to the imperious authority which his companions might sense but could never hear.

There is also an indication that Joseph must have been well informed. He provides a retreat sufficiently near one of his farms to give easy access to food and supplies but sufficiently secluded in its olive grove to give Jesus and his companions rest and tranquillity. Somehow this is not the picture of a man indulging the whim of a wayward and incomprehensible nephew. It seems more the concurring action of a man who knew something of the drama that had to be played and at least a little of his own role in it.

One speculates upon the possibility that the whole external organisation of the mission was the responsibility of the Essene school at which Jesus had received guidance.

The goatherd and his wife further up the valley acted as caretakers at one retreat. Could there be just a hint here of something behind the scenes, a watching brief unsuspected by a casual traveller in the area?

The picture of Jesus at Akka is a new glimpse reinforcing that aspect of Jesus's character on which T.P. insists before all else—the exultant vibrant human being. The "Man of Sorrows" was essentially a "Man of Joy", radiant with physical as well as spiritual energy.

At what point, one wonders, did the imitation depart so dreadfully from the example as to become in fact its polar opposite? Where in the life of this exultant vibrant Jesus is the warrant for the Puritan, the Calvinist, the Wee Free?

Could it be that in this present sketch of the personal nature of Jesus there lies the deepest, most qualitative adjustment to be made in our attitude?

Will the new dispensation restore this factor of exultant living, in which the whole of historical Christianity has been so tragically defective? Are some of the present trends towards "paganism" really imperfectly resolved effects of this impulse already working as a leaven in our current confusion?

The Passing By glimpse is one of the shortest, the simplest, perhaps the most matter of fact. Perhaps it is also one of the most significant?

CHAPTER THREE

At Supper

W.T.P. The Last Supper was by no means the strictly formal occasion which the Gospel narratives seem to suggest. It was not until the close of the meal that a ceremonial element replaced what had been till then a friendly gathering, similar to many over which Jesus had presided during the three years of his Ministry. Before the meal Jesus blessed the food and also those who were to serve it, namely the good man and his wife and their kinsman, the water carrier who had stayed on to help with the serving, and later with the washing up.

The disciples were weary and hungry after a long day's tramp over dusty tracks from Bethany. Apart from goat's milk they had not tasted food since the previous evening. Although Jesus appeared to be in an unusually serious mood when the meal began, those present seemed unaware of the momentous and tragic events that were to follow. Conversation was informal and centred on the happenings of the day, praise of the excellent food provided and speculations about the current unrest in the city, details of which their host and the water carrier had been able to give them.

The disciples talked together in small groups and from time to time went over to a serving table which stood near the door to refill their plates and cups.

A rigid vegetarian observing the scene would not have

been too happy, for the meal was by no means strictly this. It included dried fish soaked in olive oil and served with herb salad and lemon juice. The main dish consisted of rice, chicken, wild potatoes and a kind of mushroom, together with a sauce containing mint and spices. The whole was served from a large earthenware dish which stood, steaming hot, on the side table; and with the exception of Jesus, each took his platter and helped himself. The good man's wife (the hostess) herself served Jesus.

A chunk of unleavened bread (dipped first in salt water) was eaten with this main dish, the bread often replacing a fork. Wooden spoons, not knives, were used.

Dessert consisted of dried figs, nuts, raisins and a kind of guava, all served with moist goat's milk cheese. Wine and cooled drinking water were on the table in smallish jars and pitchers.

After the ceremonial partaking of the bread and wine, the cups were rinsed in water before further use. Hands were washed in a large bowl before the meal and also between courses and at the end.

During the evening the good man's wife begged Jesus for a remedy for her little girl who was in bed with a feverish chill, and Jesus directed one of the twelve, who had the hands of healing, to accompany her to the child's bedroom on the ground floor.

At the close of the meal the gathering broke up temporarily. Several of the disciples helped to clear the table, others went downstairs and in twos and threes walked to and fro in front of the house, discussing the future and wondering what the Master's intentions for the morrow were likely to be. Very soon all concerned were called back into the Upper Room. Jesus then asked for a fresh supply of bread and wine to be placed on the table; but before the ceremony of the Passover began, he had called for a bowl of water and a clean towel, and the washing of the feet took place.

Peter had already divined Jesus' intention and insisted that the disciples should go downstairs into the shed behind the kitchen, for the purpose of cleaning their feet and sandals.

The actual "washing" by Jesus was full of symbolism and he may well have been surprised to discover that the feet he "washed" were already more than usually clean!

During the bread and wine ceremony and the prophetic utterances which accompanied and followed this rite, all present stood in a circle around the table; and having partaken, each disciple knelt beside his stool and prayed in silence. Then each one rose and sat down, filled with a sense of stupefaction at what Jesus had said to Judas. Peter asked John to beg the Master to explain the meaning of his words and also to tell them whether he really expected to be arrested that very night, but Jesus remained silent. To raise their spirits, however, he began to lead them in Songs of Praise which continued from then onwards and later all the way up into the Garden.

I am often asked whether I have any reason for supposing that my descriptions of Jesus and his times is anything more than an imaginative reconstruction of what may have been the actual facts.

Why, it is asked, should credence be given to these, especially as what I write does not always conform with the

Gospel narratives even if these themselves are often contradictory in substance and in detail.

These are very pertinent queries, and they deserve frank answers. I can supply no tangible evidence in support of my conviction that these "glimpses" are not the product of imagination but are based on memory. I do not expect the reader to share this conviction because no proofs of accuracy are at present available, and also because in the present stage of our knowledge, no clear line can be drawn between the faculty of memory and the faculty of imagination.

I have spent much of my life in studying and in training to distinguish between these two faculties of the mind, both of which are our common heritage. Recollection of past events in human history is surely possible because we are the inheritors of a form of racial memory, a reservoir into which we can dip our minds from time to time. For those who believe that we are here on earth only once in our journey across Eternity, the concept that we may be able to recollect events and experiences from previous mundane existences, is of course inadmissible.

If, however, the possibility of recovering memories of past events in human history is not ruled out in connection with these writings, it is important that a note of caution should be sounded. I address this warning as much to myself as to the reader.

Ideas and the thought forms they create are the foundation of every external experience or event. Ourselves and everything we see around us could not have come into manifestation unless preceded by an Idea or a series of Ideas. The universe as a whole is founded on the principle.

AT SUPPER

The Word (the primal Idea) was proclaimed by the Creator and "There was Light".

Past happenings in human history are transitory events which come and go, leaving little or no permanent trace. The glimpses offered here are not, however, based on the recollection of such events themselves. They derive from careful study of the Ideas which preceded and caused these events to unroll in the human conditions of time and space.

This thesis presupposes the belief that mental concepts do not die and pass away, but are indelibly recorded in a manner which can be "read" or recollected, irrespective of the time interval between the event and its recovery by the trained mind of the recollector.

There is good reason, I think, to accept this statement as correct, but it should be added that whilst external events happen transitorily and then pass out of existence, the essence, the sum total effect of each event is absorbed back into the original concept or Idea that was the primary cause for bringing it into being. It is from a study of this combination of pre and post etheric records that the person recalling is able to reconstitute details of the events as they happened—as if he had been a spectator.

Accordingly it is immaterial whether or not he himself in a past life was present in bodily form on any particular occasion.

All this may sound complicated and difficult to understand, but in my view no other theory of the miracle of memory is tenable. If we consider, for instance, the possibility that the glimpses of Jesus and his times, as given in these writings, were in fact based on memory, then it is necessary to explain the source material utilised for the purpose. This source material, as already stated, is not based on a recollection of the external events or experiences described. It is based upon an *interpretation* of the Ideas which brought such events or experiences into existence.

The problem that faces the mind of the "recollector" is how to interpret, and then to convert into modern idiom, Ideas that were formulated say 2,000 years ago. This process can well lead to error arising not so much from faulty memory as from the misinterpretation of the Ideas brought back into consciousness. It is important that the significance of this warning should be fully appreciated by those who read what I have written.

I should like to say: You are endowed with the gifts of reason, intuition and instinct. All three of these should play their part in helping you to decide what is acceptable as truth for you and what is false. What I suggest is that you use these three faculties prayerfully and without bias, in order to reach your own conclusions, whether it be about what I write or about any problem or situation facing you. Nothing should ever be accepted as "truth" until you yourself secure its confirmation from within yourself and in such a way as to convert belief into certainty.

Lang: Three things will chiefly strike the reader. The first is the gentle "ordinariness" of the account. The second is the apparently minor extent to which it diverges from official versions. The third is T.P.'s concern that we read it with certain reservations.

First the ordinariness. In an important respect this could be evidence in favour of its authenticity. There is, I believe, a certain psychological technique of assessing evidence about matters which appear to extend beyond the frontiers of the five senses. It consists of a method of filtering out data which, though possibly valid, could nevertheless derive from a subconscious rearrangement of existing material. On this basis trivial data (if relevant) may have higher evidential value than data which conform to an accepted overall pattern. So I think with the Supper script. Both the incident of the child in bed with a cold and the delightful affair of Peter's fastidiousness about the unwashed feet seem to increase rather than to reduce credibility.

Both are germane, but in a certain sense irrelevant. Against the magnitude of the event suggested by the Last Supper they ring true precisely because they are not worth the trouble of inventing.

The second point is the marginal divergence from official accounts. This would seem to be a further example of an adjustment, barely significant at ordinary level but essential (if there is anything to be said for our general theory) at the level of a higher purpose which we do not perceive. It may be that T.P. does not glimpse it either, because in a letter on the subject he gives a clear impression of being in possession of something less than full understanding of his reasons for writing it. He says:

> What IS the basis of my certitude that the compilers of the Matthew and Mark gospels were wrong in inferring that the bread and wine ceremonial took place during the main meal? And that Luke was right in saying that this ceremony followed the Supper and was a separate event?
>
> And again, *vide* Luke that the Cup was offered first as a preliminary gesture and only subsequently were the

AT SUPPER

bread and wine partaken. Does it matter? Are such details important?

Lang: Here is no implicit claim to total comprehension. On the contrary almost a *cri du coeur* for a wider glimpse himself.

Perhaps more than anything hitherto, this, for me, confirms the authenticity of his glimpses. An imaginative witness tells a complete story. A witness to fact seldom does. He is too bound by his service to the truth as he has seen it.

The third point is the nature of T.P.'s faculty, which, to avoid compromise with the terminology of say, Steiner, Blavatsky or Gurdjieff we might simply call extended memory.

T.P. is much concerned to point out that in his case extended memory is fallible and should provide us with no more than the basis of an attitude, pending the time when we are able to verify it, or invalidate it, through our own exercise of the same faculty.

Attempts to make him commit himself further are apt to generate some heat. One such reaction by him is useful, however, in providing an insight into the immense difficulties inherent in the process of extended memory. It may also provide a feeling of gratitude for what he has been able to share with us.

W.T.P. "When one reaches up into the Spheres in order to grasp a fistful of ideas the results can be unexpected. One is not provided with a fluent stream of spiritualistic 'communications' but with an assortment of symbols and hieroglyphics if you like, which at first glance mean nothing. In any case they are 'negatives' which must first be developed into three dimensional positives. Quite an undertaking! Then comes the task of finding words into which the symbols can be clothed coherently. I envy those who can climb a mount, converse with a teacher, take notes and return with a fully fledged essay on God, Man and the secrets of the Universe. Even when the symbols are fully interpreted in words a further problem arises because the combinations of words to express ideas do not mean the same to those who read them, each individual's mental outlook being different. So the ideas behind the words receive varying ways of interpretation. Yes, and misinterpretation. I am interested in reaching the man in the street, leaving occult students to fend for themselves. Therefore the need arises to step down ideas to a point of simplicity which, to some, may appear to approach puerility. You pundits make scant allowance for the problems facing those to whom you direct your questions."

Lang: I have mentioned elsewhere the idea that T.P.'s work may be concerned with linking the past and the future by some sort of catalytic action in the present.

This impression was strong in relation to the Chalice Well project and just recently new developments there have reinforced it.

Adjoining the garden where the spring rises there is a sixteenth century house called Little St. Michael. For the past seven years it has been a guest house, meeting place and centre for pilgrims and visitors from all parts of the world.

AT SUPPER

Recently, the upper storey of this house was converted into one large room. Gradually the purpose for this became known, which is to create a replica, so far as this is possible, of the Upper Room in which the Last Supper was held.

I must confess that at first this plan seemed to carry a suggestion of iconolatry which I found disconcerting. However, the realisation of the project has totally dispelled this impression.

All areas of imagination and wishful thinking allowed for, it seems clear that what has taken shape in the top floor of Little St. Michael represents the external aspect of a spiritual energy so palpable that it registers (without necessarily being recognised) on quite ordinary people, even when they are unaware of what might be called the background of the situation.

Believing that the purpose of the Upper Room, whatever that purpose might be, could not be concerned *solely* with providing a link—even a revitalised link—with the impulse of a past or passing era I waited for an indication of some new factor suggesting a transition from the old to the forthcoming.

In T.P.'s talk to Companions and friends of Chalice Well in August 1967, this expectation was realised. The Upper Room, which at present represents a Supper, is shortly to have added to it an element which will symbolise a Breakfast. Here indeed is the bridging situation, the catalysis of separates. In one room will be symbolised the alchemy whereby the Aquarian and the Piscean are reconciled. Occasionally, just for an instant it IS possible to glimpse something of the magnitude of what is here represented.

Although I cannot pretend to have foreseen it, when the

plan was made public in the course of T.P.'s address there was a strange shock of familiarity. Many of us felt that we had known this all along—without realising that we knew.

Here is the relevant part of what Tudor Pole had to say.

W.T.P. "Under our guidance the whole of the top floor of Little St. Michael has been converted into one large room with the addition of several extra windows. There is an atmosphere of quiet and enlightenment already present in this Upper Room which can be felt almost tangibly by those who spend a while silently 'up there'. The Table and its thirteen stools will, we hope, be ready before long for placing in their rightful positions and the whole concept should be completed, furnishing and special lighting included later in the year.

"I have been asked to define the objects for which this 'Upper Room' has been conceived and constituted. In my view the majority of those who dwell for a time in this unique and luminous place will need no explanation from me as to the reasons for its creation. A healing Presence dwells there which can be felt by those who know how to be still and inwardly receptive, a Presence available for bringing harmony and health to those in need.

"For the rest it can be said that we have tried to create a replica, in so far as this is possible, of that wonderful Room on the outskirts of Jerusalem where Jesus met his disciples in order to partake of the Last Supper and to prepare them for the stupendous happenings that were to follow. A vivid recollection of these events in the quiet of our Upper Room can help us to prepare for our own upliftment in the sure recognition of the Master's promise that, 'I, if I be lifted up from the earth, will draw all men unto me' (St. John, xii, 32).

"But there is more that can be said. The true value of looking backward to the time when Christ's Message for Eternity was first given to the world through Jesus, nearly two thousand years ago, lies mainly in the incentive which it inspires in us to look forward and to gird ourselves anew and so to become warriors in His service this very day. A new dawn is breaking and the sun will soon be rising on a day when a breakfast meal will be prepared to which we shall be invited, one and all.

"When the darkness of the passing night is over, The Christ will lay the table and we must be ready and equipped to share breakfast with Him. The Upper Room at Chalice Well will have its part to play, even if only as a symbol of a great event in times which may be nearer than we dare imagine.

"When meditating, therefore, in the room that Chalice Well has provided, whether there in person or in thought, let your minds turn from the memory of the Last Supper towards the Breakfast that is destined to follow in its wake. In this way we shall be helped to prepare for future service in the spirit of the prayer:

> *May Thy Will be done on earth,*
> *Show me how to do my part.*

"In due course and as at present advised, a second table will be laid for 'breakfast' at the end of the Upper Room, facing the gardens and the orchards, with Michael's Tor on the horizon; and it is across this scene that the rising sun will cast its radiance."

AT SUPPER

Lang: Here then is a remarkable sequence of events. Sixty-three years ago T.P. saw a few acres of land in Somerset and realised that over and over again in past history it had been concerned with what might be called the Impulse of Renewal. Half a century later he was instrumental in buying this property and securing it in perpetual trust. To this place and the house associated with it, people have been drawn from all over the world; and now, gradually, further aspects of what appears to be a master plan are falling into place. There is a finesse about it, an expertise, as though parts of a jigsaw picture were assuming their proper place each at its rightful position and at exactly the moment allowed for.

But it would be wrong to feel that all is predestined, certain, free from contingency. It may be that if there is a master plan, it exists in perfect entirety. But the task of working out its external realisation is certainly not predetermined, at least not in the same way. The labour in the field is all too subject to error, accident and disappointment.

To correct any possible impression that the Chalice Well Occasion (to use a Sufi term) is assured at some higher level and needs only acceptance and approval here below I should like to give one anecdote which clearly illustrates the reverse. At ordinary level, the components of the Occasion have to be assembled in very human conditions of difficulty, frustration, and it may be, failure.

As a preface to what follows it may be advisable to prepare the reader for something a little out of the ordinary.

Those who know Tudor Pole's book *The Silent Road* will be familiar with the fact that he enjoys the periodic attention of what in other days would probably have been called a Good Fairy. The idea that a human being can communicate with a kind of being having a lesser degree of materiality than ours and belonging to a different order of evolution is securely authenticated by folklore. Since the Middle Ages the reality (which was not uncommon then and is not uncommon now) became gradually masked in suggestive symbolism. At the present time there is no way by which the fact—and it is a fact—can be conveyed without affront to what we mistakenly regard as our sophisticated scientific cosmology.

Tudor Pole has got round this simply by being out and out unabashed. He refers to "a little friendly genie" and leaves you to smile condescendingly if you feel like it. If what follows goes beyond modern boundaries of the credible, then disregard it. Assume it is an aspect of human imagination, but absorb the facts of the rest. For facts they are.

This is the story as he told it to me.

W.T.P. "I sought a table for our Upper Room which would be as near as possible a replica. In the original, the top was made of olive wood, finely fashioned and grained, but the legs and supports came from the yew tree, olive wood being too soft for this purpose. As you know, the good man of the house was a master carpenter and expert craftsman in wood and he knew how to select the best materials for his purpose. Soon after he married, he made a table specially designed and dedicated for ceremonial use at the Passover and on one or two other Hebrew festival anniversaries. Being an instinctive seer, he felt from the first that the table he was making would be used one day for a great purpose beyond his comprehension. For this reason he chose the wood with immense care and put all his loving reverence into the task of fashioning an object of simple but perfect beauty.

"Impossible therefore to do more than create a symbolical replica under modern Western conditions. The original table would seat thirteen and was about eight feet long by three feet. On Passover occasions there were usually gathered about a dozen of the good man's friends and relatives including himself, his wife and an unmarried sister of hers; later on his two children, a boy and a girl. The table came to fruition soon after his son and heir was born and the attic room was then redesigned to make it fitting for use on special occasions (stools were used, but only one was made with a back rest for use by the giver of the feast. These seemed to be made of pear wood and finely matched). Wondering how to proceed, my little familiar 'genie' appeared on the scene. 'The nearest approach to what you seek can be found in a cellar not far distant from the London hotel you frequent . . .' (in ideographs, not words).

"And so I set out from the St. Ermin's Hotel to scour side streets in the immediate neighbourhood. But how to spot the cellar referred to seemed hopeless. Finally I came across a furniture depository and in I went, to be met with: 'A table such as you describe is unobtainable; especially as you rule out oak and mahogany. However, come in and look around'; which I then did to no useful purpose. 'Have you a cellar?' 'We have an underground storage department which was once a series of cellars and passages. Come down if you like and look around.' Down we went into a labyrinth of coiled stairways and cellar rooms, all crammed with furniture and junk. Finally in a dark recess I spotted a lengthy shape which called out to me and I asked for a light. And there was revealed the table of my dreams or as near as makes no difference, simple in design but superb in its aura. Dimensions eight feet by three feet standing on simply carved legs of yew wood: The top was certainly not made of olive wood but of a lovely grained fruit wood, probably cherry. To my mind, and as a lover of choice woods, something out of this world. A dream come true.

" 'How has this lovely piece been overlooked?' I asked. Commotion followed and several assistants were called down to a conference carried on beyond my hearing. Finally: 'Oh yes, we are able to offer you this table but it is unique, or almost so, and by no means cheap.' (I don't believe they knew it was there.) Further conferences, then: 'This is early seventeenth century and of English make, almost certainly, and we know of nothing else like it. The price is £675!'

"I sat down on a nearby stool and metaphorically wept. Then in fury I turned on my genie saying in effect: 'What on earth was the use of your leading me here when you must have known that my limit was £250?' This testy remark received the scathing reply, as follows: 'I have succeeded in finding what you sought and money is no concern of mine.' And off he went in a huff. Naturally, I was left in deep frustration.'

Lang: No clear assessment of this episode seems possible. You take it or leave it. But it is not without interest that in his next letter he said: "One of the foremost wood craftsmen in England has just telephoned unexpectedly offering his services if I decide to have a table made."

The focus of the ceremony that took place in the original Upper Room was the Chalice or Cup. Possibly no other object holds such significance in the entire body of Christian belief. T.P. believes that this was not a cup as normally understood, but a shallow vessel like a deep saucer.

He believes that this vessel was dipped into a large Chalice containing the wine and was then passed round.

When not in use it rested on a stand consisting of a base and a stem so that when vessel and stand were nested together the whole had the appearance of a goblet.

What happened to this vessel after it had fulfilled its sacred purpose? "Genuine relics" of Christian Events have abounded through the ages and still do. "Fragments of the true Cross" financed many a medieval monastery.

In *A Man Seen Afar*, T.P. indicates that the Cross (and the other two crosses) did not survive. He describes their destruction by fire; and the subsequent vision vouchsafed to Joseph of Arimathea.

However, did any other article irradiated with the vibrations of Jesus survive? Is it possible that the Cup of the Last Supper still exists? Has Tudor Pole been permitted any insight in this connection? Attempts to extract a clear declaration from him fail. It may be that he knows the answer but is not permitted to reveal it. On the whole it is perhaps safer to assume that he does not know beyond doubt. But it is safe to assume that he has good reason to suspect a link between the Cup of the Last Supper and an object at present in his possession.

I refer to the Glastonbury Vessel, the existence of which

is known to a small circle of people in Europe and America. This object, a description of which follows in T.P.'s own words, is one of the most mysterious ever to escape widespread publicity.

It was found in St. Bride's Well, at Glastonbury in 1906. It might be more accurate to say that it found itself, because there is some suggestion that its presence was revealed to T.P.'s clairvoyance. It was actually recovered by his sister and two of her friends under T.P.'s directions.

Its external mystery consists in this. Nothing comparable to it is known in any museum in the world. Its type, material and workmanship suggest that it was possibly made by a glassworker in the region of Antioch very long ago. However, if this were so its vitreous surface would give certain indications recognisable to experts. These are either absent or contradictory. On the other hand, if its manufacture were as recent as its surface texture suggests under microscopic examination, there is no parallel for the manufacture of an article of such workmanship in modern times.

So it HAS to be recent, but it isn't; and it MUST be old but it can't be!

Its inner mystery consists in the powerful effect which it has on sensitives of all kinds. The glimpses of the life and times of Jesus which T.P. published in *A Man Seen Afar* were largely due to sensing the atmosphere which surrounds this vessel.

Nor is such an effect exclusive to him. One sensitive knowing nothing whatever of this blue sapphire bowl began to describe a scene in which thirteen figures sat at a long table. She felt that she was witnessing a picture of the Last Supper, but when, on a later occasion, she saw this bowl (which without her knowledge had in the meantime been turned half round), she stated that she perceived the same scene but this time in profile.

The vessel has been in Tudor Pole's possession since it was brought to light sixty years ago.

To "explain" it from any point of view seems hopeless. He has never suggested that it is the Cup of the Last Supper (which legend says was brought to Glastonbury by Joseph of Arimathea). He has never explicitly said that it is not. Could it have been dematerialised for centuries and reconstituted when the occasion was right? Is this the explanation of the fact that it is both very old and very new?

Such a speculation is made in modern times at the risk of ridicule. Yet T.P. has had personal experience of such an "impossibility" three times in his life, once involving a ring, once a piece of jewellery and once involving *himself*.

One day, after being near to the vessel for some time I mentioned my surprise that such an object should exist in a private house with no special precaution against theft.

Another historical relic which possesses—or is believed to possess—energies of a high order has been the object of attention by certain individuals and groups on different occasions throughout the centuries.

The relic to which I refer was the focus of a carefully planned secret operation in the year 875 when it was obtained by a trick from its rightful custodian and taken to southern Sicily. Its employment to raise power unlawfully was thwarted at the last moment by the self sacrifice of a holy (and knowledgeable) person. This same relic was stolen for the second time a thousand years later (on March 13th, 1938) and attempts made to use it to raise

AT SUPPER

power for a group working for the success of the Nazi ideology.

Its secretion in Nurenburg, its burial in a secret hiding place and its recovery soon after the death of Hitler is one of the strangest stories of World War Two.

I had related this story to T.P. and implied concern that the Glastonbury vessel might one day attract similar attention. T.P. shook his head and said very firmly, "This is one of the comparatively few objects which carries perfect protection within itself."

Here follows his own account of the Vessel and all he apparently wishes to say about it.

THE CUP OF PEACE

This is a small and fairly shallow blue sapphire bowl, made from crystalline substance and containing floral milleflori designs in blue, green and amber. The flower pattern is interlined by silver-leaf foil of perfect lustre.

A detailed description of this unique vessel's manufacture was prepared by the late Sir William Crookes, F.R.S., the famous chemist who was also a glass expert in his own right. He gave it as his opinion, in conversation with W.T.P. in 1908 that this remarkable object was not of modern construction, in spite of its comparatively good state of preservation.

Mr. J. Reed, the British Museum glass expert of that time agreed with this view. Some other glass experts do not share his opinion in this respect and believe that this vessel is probably comparatively modern, despite certain flaws and erosion which would suggest the contrary.

No other glass object, similar or actually identical with

this one has ever been found, in spite of prolonged research throughout the contents of the world's museums and private collections.

This "blue sapphire bowl" came to light under unusual circumstances in 1906, when it was discovered beneath flat stones at the base of a water source then known as St. Bride's Well, Glastonbury. This Well is no longer in existence due to extensive irrigation works undertaken at and around this spot some twenty-five years ago. This site was situated about a mile west of the Abbey ruins on the inner bank of the Brue stream and was overshadowed, until its destruction, by a wide spreading Thorn tree of considerable age and beauty.

In comparatively recent times an engraved stone was erected not far from the spot where the Well once stood.

No one knows for how long this vessel, thickly caked with mud when found, had lain in St. Bride's Well prior to 1906.

On July 3rd, 1965, a group of antiquarians and museum experts met at Wells, Somerset, for the main purpose of examining this vessel. Opinions as to its age and origin were divided in view of the fact that none of those present had ever seen a similar object with which this bowl could be compared.

Since its discovery in 1906 this vessel has remained in the possession of W.T.P., his sister, K.T.P., and two friends who were connected with bringing it to light (the Misses Janet and Christine Allen). Many remarkable healings and visions have been associated with it and the atmosphere around it appears to be one of peace and sanctity of a special character and to which many people have testified.

A permanent resting place for this unique object has

been prepared in the Upper Room at Little St. Michael, Chalice Well.

It is far from the intention of those concerned that this vessel shall be placed on view as an object for veneration or as a relic to be revered in its own right. On the other hand it should be regarded as an important symbol of unity and brotherhood, a reminder of the great purposes to which the Master Jesus consecrated the Cup of the Last Supper. It can and should also be regarded as the insignia of the New Era now approaching, when the Cup will replace the Cross as the sign manual of the single and universal Faith destined to lead Humanity forward toward the ultimate goal of the Golden Age.

CHAPTER FOUR

The Word

Lang: In an attempt to draw together all of the subject matter I had received from T.P. I began to submit this and that tentative conclusion and this and that leading question to him.

The results were always unexpected. Sometimes it was correction that came; sometimes endorsement; sometimes wholly new material that often seemed irrelevant. What did emerge was that specific ideas submitted to him produce specific responses which are on the whole "harder", more unequivocal, than material which originates spontaneously from his own intention.

Gradually a picture began to emerge which could be seen as consisting of a number of sections: errors in Christian belief that have grown up because of (and sometimes in spite of) the Gospels; the humanity of Jesus, as distinct from the Christ spirit overshadowing him; the effect of the Hebraic tradition of prophecy on the Christian message; and lastly the nature of the Impulse of Renewal which is now both imminent and actual.

All really converges on the last idea which conveys the view that an immense flow of cosmic energy is now in process of penetrating human consciousness to become available for human enlightenment. This is not to be regarded as an allegorical event, related to a distant, possible future. It is actual, tangible and immediate. It is happening in our lifetime, here and now. Everything that T.P. has seen and handed on—however apparently oblique and tangential—is in fact directly aligned on this. When this new energy has suffused the planet we can expect a transformation unimaginable in terms of all existing ideas. This is to come, yet it is also here and now. How to resolve this paradox?

If we look at the historical record, we can see, over and over again, that each "month" of the great zodiacal year has possessed its own distinctive character, a signature as it were, for the fiat which authorises and inspires a new phase in the evolutionary process.

We can look back to an era when men were impelled, subtly but imperiously, to disperse and search. We can—even more clearly—see the record of another era when men were impelled to congregate, to concentrate their cultures, to Build. We have seen the most recent era when man was impelled to see himself as self sufficient and the centre of as much of the universe as he could discern with his external senses.

The arrival of each of these eras produced explosions shattering the standards and acceptances of the existing order. All of them in their initial stages must have been violently uncomfortable. Yet all seem to have had a beginning and an end. There is no seeming sanction for the idea that an impulse of this kind can be both potential and actual at the same time. Yet that, in connection with the Aquarian impulse is what T.P. appears to be saying.

Here is his explanation.

THE WORD

W.T.P. Jesus descended into the realms of human consciousness over a period of nearly a century before he appeared in bodily form. Seers within the ranks of the Essenes were able during that prior period of approach "to pick up" and inscribe on scrolls, fragments from the message Jesus was destined to impart during his ministry on earth.

This fact explains the seeming mystery of how, for instance, teaching to be given later on the Mount was received and recorded many years before "A.D." dawned. Esoteric records can show a similar procedure before the physical birth of great Messengers from God throughout the ages.

It is my belief that the "Revealer of the Word" (the "Christos") for the historic times in which we now live, has already descended into the invisible spheres that surround our planet and that those with eyes to see and ears to hear, can begin to discern the Message he is bringing, even if the Messenger may not be clothed in form or outwardly discernible.

Our Elder Brothers, carriers of the imprimatur of the eternal Christ, usually come among us quietly and unannounced. No glare of spiritual trumpets heralds their arrival. We should not presume to predict the time or circumstances of an event, which in any case is dependent on factors far beyond our comprehension; but each awakening soul, according to his vision and capacity, can help to prepare the way.

We can "look within" and bring forth the *Word*, the Christos, waiting to be awakened from within the citadel of our own being.

During the present century "Preparers of the Way"

have lived among us, sometimes quite unknown, sometimes the visible exponents of facets of truth, forerunners of the Revealer of the Word. Their lives and actions have created a leaven in human consciousness, a leaven that has caused tumults and disturbances fostered by both human karmic conditions and (to use a symbolic term) by the "Energies of the Left". But the Light has pierced our darkness and we can all help to reflect this Light in our own lives and pass it on. By doing so, in however humble a manner, we too can claim to be counted among the Preparers of the Way.

Whether the Revealer of the Word is already embodied in form (unrecognised) as some assert, is of secondary importance. Whether such an Advent is near or to be delayed or even to be postponed indefinitely is also of only relative importance.

What is supremely significant for us to realise is that the Word itself is in our midst here and now, *potentialised* in such a way as to meet the needs of the present hour in human destiny, available to you and to me and all mankind, waiting to come into manifestation from within ourselves.

The immediate imminence of this truth is for us to grasp and utilise NOW.

Expectation that we may be nearing a manifestation of the divine purpose for our time and age is not confined to Christians and Jews, but is also prevalent among Moslems, Hindus, Buddhists, and followers of many other oriental faiths. This expectation may be partly aroused by the widespread realisation that the use of man's freewill in negative and destructive directions is bringing the human race and all life on this planet to the edge of grave disaster. The cry goes up for "*Help*"!

THE WORD

What can ordinary people like ourselves do in face of such a situation? We can pray and we can think and act constructively in our daily lives and we can learn how to become spiritually perceptive. We can resist being carried away by the clamour of those who predict either catastrophe on the one hand or phenomenal apparitions in the skies accompanied by cosmic fireworks on the other; or those who give "dates" for and descriptions of an Advent, such descriptions being based largely on psychic imagination.

St. John begins his Gospel with the very enigmatical statement that "In the beginning was the Word and the Word was with God, and the Word was God".

To human sense a word is an external symbol for expressing an idea. We can only suppose that the true meaning of the Logos or Word can be interpreted as being the embodiment or expression of Divinity in a supreme Idea, containing within itself the essence of all Wisdom, all Love and all Life, just as the seed of an oak contains in potency the whole tree. If this be correct then it would follow that the whole of creation stemmed from a Thought or an Idea in the Mind of the Creator. We can only surmise that the gradual unfoldment of this central Idea is embodied in what we call evolution.

Later in the same chapter St. John speaks of the Word having become flesh through the mysterious event associated with the overshadowing of Jesus by the Christ. This creative Word therefore is now enshrined in Man himself, whose task it is to bring it out into the light of day, through his every thought, word and deed.

Soon now a realisation will dawn among us which will enable it to be said with knowledge and conviction that

THE WORD

"In the present is the Word and the Word is with Man and the Word *is* Man". The truth expressed in this statement presages the ultimate transformation of mortal man into divine man, made in the image and likeness of God.

We do not know how this creative Word or Idea is likely to be manifested in our time and age. Almost certainly we can expect teaching that will give us fuller understanding of the meaning of life, its origin and purpose, the reasons for our presence here, where we have come from and what our future is to be. Hitherto such knowledge has never been disclosed to us authoritatively in such a way as to reach the understanding of the common man. Now the time has come for such a revelation, one that will do much to advance the spiritual and moral progress of the race.

We are told that "In the Beginning" God spoke, saying "Let there be Light" and there was Light, this being the first time that the creative Word was used. No human terms are available in which to describe the mystery of Creation, but it would seem evident that it was from within this Light that Life itself first appeared. Life, being eternal, had no beginning in terms of time and space, but the utterance of the Word brought about the clothing of Life in Light and then in form. The uses made by Life of the many forms embodying it on every level of being created the conditions through which Intelligence became individualised and began its ever expanding development, a process that will continue even when the need for bodily form has disappeared.

We should take courage from the realisation that we are indeed children of the Light and owe our very existence to that fact. We may use our energies in wrong directions by plunging down into the darkness, which the gift of freewill enables us to do, but the Light within us can never be extinguished and its ultimate triumph is assured beyond the shadow of any doubt or seeming obstacle.

It is my belief that the Revealer of the Word who now approaches human levels, whether he is to be clothed in visible form or not, will bring with him the inspiration and the spiritual impetus we need in order to lift human consciousness out of its present darkness into the Light of new Day. One thing is certain. If we are to equip ourselves to receive and understand the Revealer, the coming Messenger from God, we must arouse ourselves from sleep and prepare ourselves for this arrival.

We must become freed from dwelling blindly within the confines of the immediate present, circumscribed and to a large extent unaware of who we are and of the cosmic purposes for our existence. No longer should the belief persist that Life has either a beginning or an ending, or that it can be destroyed. The word "death" is deadly in its implications and the thraldom of belief in it must cease. Life can change its forms a myriad times and in a myriad ways, but it can never be extinguished. It is the exernal gift of the Creator to us all and no power in heaven or on earth can deprive us of it. May the Revealer of the Word in his own time and his own way bring this Truth home to us and so banish the fear of "death", that great illusion, for ever from our minds, our hearts and our lives.

Lang: The statement that Jesus descended into human spheres nearly a century before he appeared in bodily form is an illuminating one. Here in a single sentence is the explanation of the conflict that has so harassed Bible scholars. They have held, very rightly, to the emotional conviction that the Advent and its message was unique in all history. At the same time they were confronted with documentary proof in so many manuscripts that it was nothing of the kind. In their hearts the Bible scholars knew that what Jesus brought was new. In their heads they had to admit that it already existed before he arrived.

At the level of logic the impasse is absolute. Yet by raising consciousness one dimension the impossibles are reconciled—seen in fact never to have been in conflict.

One wonders how many tenets of Christian belief so stubbornly and so long at issue with the facts of human experience await a similar effortless resolution. So often we are told that black and white, positive and negative, exclusive and inclusive seem irreconcilable only because of our human polar thinking; that at a higher level opposites are reconciled. But how very seldom do we discover this truth in an actual tangible example. This surely is one such and should be prized accordingly.

It is clear from what T.P. says that the new Impulse is already oxygenating the turgid waters of our twentieth-century life, but he is less forthcoming on the question of whether the Impulse will take embodiment soon, later or at all.

It is perhaps possible to glimpse something of the transformation of human life which could result from the new Impulse.

W.T.P. Almost certainly we can expect teaching that will give us fuller understanding of the meaning of life, its origin and purpose, the reasons for our presence here, where we have come from and what our future is to be.

Lang: In short a new Gnosis.

It is clear from everyday experience that a large number of ordinary people, essentially decent, benevolent and in a real sense, good seed are indifferent to Christianity precisely because it has seemingly slight intellectual content. They are willing to concede that its message is sublime but they feel that its relevance is to a phase in human development when emotion ruled and intellect was still, in the modern sense, unborn. However indignant the protests of good Christians, this is a proper complaint and it is often uttered with great humility and sincerity. Somehow there is a rightness about the idea that the nature of the new Impulse should match the nature of the humanity which needs it.

W.T.P. Hitherto such knowledge has not been disclosed to us authoritatively in such a way as to reach the common man. Now the time has come for such a Revelation. . . .

Lang: Suppose that in some way, large numbers of people could become aware of the reality of higher levels and could, step by step, glimpse the laws that interpenetrate these levels and ours. If ordinary people were increasingly to find such awareness in themselves would not a total change in human life, qualitative and utterly fundamental follow?

Signs that this is actually happening are not lacking. Alongside an enormously increased intellectual interest in what used to be called ultimate questions, there is evidence of increased sensitivity among ordinary people. Generally this does not involve those who have been interested in such matters all their lives and who have now begun to experience the first flashes of awareness and insight. It is something much more remarkable. It is the increasing incidence of sensitivity—often alarming and bewildering—among people who have never prospected in this direction at all and who have no background against which to evaluate it.

Suppose this were a mutation of the mind of humanity: suppose it were the first tentative access on a large scale to a wholly new function, whereby ordinary man is destined to be simultaneously aware of another world while living firmly in this one. There can be no statistical proof that this is happening, but it has been recorded with surprise by individuals and groups all over the world who have been led to expect such a phenomenon and who now can hardly dare to believe that it is happening.

It is an intoxicating prospect.

If it took place over a wide enough section of the human race would it not lead almost inevitably to a solution for most human ills? Would it be possible for people having access to higher levels of consciousness, and glimpsing higher laws still to manifest as wilful and savage children? It seems unlikely.

The desperate deadlock which exists in human affairs at the present time is due to the fact that human intellect understands quite clearly that it is helpless to solve the problems of its own making.

But suppose that human intellect could be irradiated by spiritual energies. Would man not be impelled to direct the powers of his mind to the new goals revealed by the spirit? Would he not rush eagerly and willingly to the task of putting the house of humanity in order?

That the new Impulse should be concerned with a new Gnosis seems entirely to be expected. The prospect is that it may be closer than we think.

Can we discern anything else that will be incorporated in the New Impulse? Almost certainly a bridge between the living and the after-life state.

T.P. believes that for much of the material of his teaching, Jesus drew almost exclusively on the Hebrew tradition; and this was—considering its Eastern origins—quite remarkably unilluminating about details of human survival. One could of course argue that Jesus deliberately confined himself, for reasons unknown to us, not to *teaching* about survival but to demonstrating it in person. Or might it be that such teaching as he did give has not come down to us?

W.T.P. Hebrew sources had, and have, little to tell us, for instance, about the conditions surrounding the death of the body and how to prepare for this all important experience. The after life is pictured as falling into three compartments, namely heaven, hell and some form of nothingness. Jesus seems to have provided no information about the conditions to be faced when we pass hence, with the result that the majority of human beings arrive "over there", unequipped, uninformed, bewildered and usually deeply distressed on finding themselves, not in "heaven" but in a condition of being in many ways little different from those they have just left. The reasons for this absence of information on a subject of such vital importance are obscure. Jesus' hearers were simple folk, mainly peasants, often illiterate, and who could only grasp the simplest exposition of the purpose and meaning of life, either here or hereafter. One could argue that the time was not ripe 2,000 years ago for filling in the gaps in order to give the intelligent man some clear idea of Whither? What? Jesus' recorded references to Heaven and the after life were nebulous, allegorical and obscure. More so in fact than the teaching provided by some of his oriental predecessors.

Now that the time has come for the Word to be proclaimed anew, we may expect clear revelations on the problems of life and death. What an immense incentive to human progress and enlightenment will result, if the gaps in our information about these matters can be filled authoritatively in reasonable detail and in ways that will transform and illumine human thinking and human acting! We are reaching another turning point in human and planetary history, perhaps a still more important one than any that has gone before, and almost certainly of greater import even than the turning point which resulted from Jesus' use of his Sword of Light. Once more the primary Rhythm is to be quickened and heightened, an event gratefully to be welcomed, even if its primary effect will be to shake our planet to its foundations.

CHAPTER FIVE

The Problem of Prophecy

Lang: I have mentioned earlier my belief that T.P. has a mission to effect certain adjustments in our picture of the historical Jesus and also in the attitudes and beliefs that have followed in consequence. I have mentioned the possibility that this cannot be done without a certain erosion of beliefs long held perhaps as articles of faith in the "common law" of Christianity, irrespective of denomination.

A distinction between Jesus and the Christos which overlighted him; certain suggestions that the Christian message as it has come down to us is incomplete; certain remarks about the dubious value of prophecy; all this leads on to dangerous territory which used to be labelled heresy. It is, however, territory which in the present context cannot in honesty be left unexplored.

W.T.P. There were occasions when it appeared that Jesus spoke from two separate levels of consciousness, his own and that of the overshading Christos, leaving his hearers to surmise which was which. He himself never proclaimed that he was the one and only son of the Father but insisted that we are all sons of God. Surely it was the Christ speaking through Jesus who announced that "I and the Father are one"? Jesus never indicated that his human birth differed from the natural one or that he—the man, though perfect in his humanity—was the saviour of the world with power to destroy all sin and evil. Doubtless it was for the purpose of making converts that the doctrines of the Virgin Birth and the idea that Jesus himself in human form was God incarnate, omnipotent and supreme arose.

Lang: T.P.'s writings usually appear to me to be concerned with the need to cause no affront to accepted ideas, however much at variance these may be with what he himself believes. But, asked bluntly about some specific question, he seems willing to answer freely and incisively.

I had detected a possibly heretical idea once or twice in relation to his views on the nature of God and Jehovah.

What emerges is that Jesus was in the habit of using the terminology of the Hebrew tradition and, on occasion, *appeared* to equate God the universal Father with the Jewish Jehovah. Jesus did not seem to take adequate steps to prevent misunderstandings arising in this respect.

The equating of Jehovah with the Absolute is to T.P. a grave error of interpretation and one which has troubled the Christian stream for two thousand years. The unequivocal declaration that the Hebrew conception of Jehovah is not a true picture of God the supreme Creator of the universe, and the replacement of this misconception by the truth as Jesus really taught it to his disciples, is perhaps one of the conditions upon which the ground may be prepared for the Aquarian seed to fructify.

In T.P.'s treatment of this, an extremely important idea emerges. It is that when psychic mental energies are sufficiently concentrated, a delusive entity may be formulated which can have endurance in time and which may manifest as though it were actually alive. It becomes a thought form with power to act, as if on its own volition.

Here is what T.P. says:

W.T.P. Jesus spoke of his Father in terms of omnipotent love and wisdom yet he seems to have done little to divert attention from the belief that the tribal god of the Jews (a most unpleasant and bloodthirsty person) was the supreme creator of the universe. The tribal god thesis, held for several thousand years and to some extent still current, has created a very dangerous situation. A thought form of immense proportions has been built up on etheric levels. The erroneous concepts of Deity held throughout such a lengthy period of time have imbued this thought form with a life and activity of its own.

This man-made "God" appears capable of intervening in planetary and human affairs in ways that are distinctly devolutionary. Inspired by Old Testament prophecies, this embodiment of human concepts seems to possess the power to intervene in the affairs of "the Chosen People" and to bring about wars and revolutions for this purpose. This embodiment appears able to create conditions favourable to the fulfilment of Old Testament predictions concerning external events said to come into being at the "end of the world" or at the close of the present age. The dangers of this menace are well known at cosmic levels and a struggle to destroy this very powerful "thoughtform" or to transmute its influence occupies the strenuous attention of our Elder Brothers. Complete success in this field depends on our co-operation. The bubble must be pricked, the concept of a tribal god imbued with his own powers destroyed and man should free himself from a dangerous entanglement once and for all. It is an entanglement that has long delayed human progress and spiritual unfoldment.

Lang: Suppose for a moment that this idea is valid; that an ancient eastern tribe, informed and expert in arcane matters—perhaps from contact with the Secret Doctrine in Babylon—had created a thought form powerfully invested with their own psychic energies. Presuming that this "elemental" exists even now: is there any reason why such an image, graven in the racial mind, should have any actual power in this modern nuclear age?

Assume that a nomadic nation had created for itself a potent thought-form continually reinforced by devotions and aspirations. Prophecy in this context would be the wish fulfilment of a people, and not the realisation of a spiritual impulse. Yet it was into such a climate of traditional belief that Jesus appeared and in this context his words were heard.

Doubtless Jesus fully understood this, but apparently no adequate steps were taken to prevent misunderstanding. Is it possible that Jesus the man was at times unable to extricate himself wholly from his own racial background? On some occasions did he take certain actions because he felt impelled to fulfil Jewish prophecy?

Here is what T.P. has to say on the subject and on the question of prophecy in general.

THE PROBLEM OF PROPHECY

W.T.P. To me Jesus' attitude and actions appear sometimes to be difficult to understand. As a man his outlook on the human scene was in a way provincial. He was proud of his Jewish descent and made full use of the sayings of the Hebrew prophets, to the point of regarding the fulfilment of their predictions as being infallible. His hearers seemed to have been given no glimpse, by quotation or otherwise of ancient wisdom, or if that is too strong a term, of the accumulated spiritual knowledge provided by his predecessors, the Masters and sages of the past. It might be argued that his teaching included in essence this spiritual knowledge, but the records that have come down to us make it permissible to infer that as a man, Jesus' historic vision drew its inspiration principally from Hebrew sources.

Was it that a sense of partial failure made him determined at all costs to "fulfil prophecy", to bring about his own death and so convert seeming failure into a measure of achievement?

Pilate was willing and ready to save him, but Jesus prevented this, mainly by arousing the passions of the Sanhedrin and the Jewish priests. Jesus appeared to be deliberately provocative when referring to the Temple's destruction and in his outspoken references to himself, designed by him to ensure conviction. To the onlooker there was something artificial about these methods which is not easy to understand.

It is a strange, sad fact that prophecy, often of a fatalistic and sombre character has always been one of the main planks in the platform of the Hebrew faith; sadder still that use of prophecy as a method for trying to reform Mankind seeped through into the Christian Era and to some extent is still with us. Non-fulfilment in a literal sense of confident forecasts timed to materialise before the passing of a single generation created dissension, disillusionment and despair among many of Jesus' early followers. We should bear these facts in mind when trying to assess the value of spectacular predictions in this field which are receiving so much credence and publicity today. The curious concept that salvation and destruction are linked inevitably together, like two sides of the same coin, appears to be a tenet of Hebrew theology, which is found nowhere else in the world scriptures.

There is no evidence from recorded history to suggest that human nature can be bettered or reformed by threats of fire and brimstone, said to be awaiting most of us in some future state of being. The ancient religions of the Far Orient rarely seem to have felt the need to include prophecy in their philosophies or predictions concerning future events on earth and in the heavens. In my view this fact deserves our serious consideration. Based largely on carefully chosen utterances from the Old Testament, interpreted through psychic communications, some of our modern soothsayers are predicting that the Age now closing is to be accompanied by disasters on such a global scale that unless a higher Power directly intervenes, hope of survival for the human race is remote. Cassandras are engaged in creating sinister thought-forms in human consciousness of a kind that tend to prevent the flames of truth from penetrating into the hearts and minds of men. Do such people ever stop to realise what deadly harm can result from their activities?

Whether they know it or not, they are playing the Devil's game and if we are not careful both they and we shall need to suffer serious consequences. Even if these dreary prophets believe their own predictions, is it not their duty, as it is ours, to put up a determined fight against the fatalism that emanates from the dank vaults of darkness and despair?

A gentle old lady, "Christian" in outlook through and through, who would not harm a fly, assured me recently that the "Coming of the Lord" would be preceded by events of a horrifying character. A vast earthquake would engulf Palestine and its people, the "Egyptians" would be destroyed and terrors unspeakable would stalk the earth. (Here again emerges the totally mistaken belief that destruction and salvation—the lost and the saved—are processes destined to take place simultaneously, and at a particular moment in human history.) I asked this good lady whether under such circumstances it was not our duty to supplicate the Deity to postpone the "Coming" until better conditions could be arranged for Our Lord's reception? This most reasonable suggestion was met by a stern rebuke and I was told that "God knows best", which of course is true. This being so, what can we gain by trying to interpret the intentions of Divinity or by searching the skies for signs and omens of what our future may hold in store? Is our faith so feeble that we can no longer live the day to the best of our ability but needs must try to anticipate tomorrow? It is useful to remind those who seek for external signs and wonders that intervention from spiritual sources in human affairs never takes the form of spectacular apparitions, but unfolds naturally, ceaselessly and in hidden ways. The seeds containing fruitful promise for our enlightenment are sown in the soil of human consciousness in an ever extending sequence and what I believe we are witnessing now is an acceleration of this process. It is a process which calls for our active and discerning co-operation because "salvation" by compulsion lies outside the orbit of the Divine plan and purpose.

Life in time and form may come and go, and the misuse of Man's free will can bring with it most unpleasant consequences, but life itself is indestructible and what we call "death" is a figment of the human imagination.

Spiritual optimism is a gift from the Gods and we should cherish this gift above pearls and with the conviction that as children of the One Father we can go forward on our ways cheerfully and without fear.

After what I have been saying you will not expect me to indulge in predictions about the future course of world events. Take courage and consolation from the fact that infinity has no boundaries in "time" and "space". All eternity is at man's disposal for fulfilment of the purposes for which he was conceived and brought into being. If we are now facing what seems to us to be a periodical fluctuation in human progress, what of it? Over the centuries the tides come in and out, but their ebb and flow are an essential part of the cosmic plan and should cause us no alarm. Storm clouds and tornadoes obscure the sun from time to time but these, too, are divine agencies, designed for our ultimate well being. Creation itself is an ever expanding process. The Universe is not static. It never ceases to unfold and we with it, and this continuing unfoldment is what we call evolution.

The creative Word, herald of a fresh Dispensation, forerunner to recognition of the Presence, is with us *now*. . . .

THE PROBLEM OF PROPHECY

Lang: From many scattered threads concerning the role of prophecy, the Jewish Jehovic tradition and the life of Jesus, it may be possible to draw some sort of tentative pattern. First: Jesus appeared unable to clarify the distinction between himself and the overshadowing Principle of the Christ sufficiently to influence the subsequent developments of theology. He appeared to make no adequate distincting between Jehovah and God the Father. Thus a series of mistaken beliefs have emerged, which have been held as truth for over two thousand years.

A radical change in outlook is now in progress. So far it has been a relatively gentle process but its tempo is increasing and at its climax it may be drastic. Here is T.P.'s comment:

W.T.P. The crumbling away of crystallised and institutional theology and dogma is a gradual process in order to avoid the creation of a vacuum. The process is now being accelerated in order that the tribal god myth may be removed from the minds of men as a preliminary to formulating in human consciousness a conception of Deity clothed in the universality of the one, all pervading, all powerful mind of the creative Principle.

It is on this conception that the foundations can be laid for a faith unshackled to outworn formulae and outgrown beliefs. The drawing together of the philosophies of East and West, freed from the man-made accretions of the centuries can only come into its own as the institutional barriers between the churches, temples and synagogues disappear in the light of a new Dispensation, created to meet the needs of humanity at this turning point in its history.

The process may involve the disappearance of denominational religion and the destruction of orthodox theology but we can look to the utterance of the Word anew to quicken the cleansing process and so bring man out into the sunlight once again.

Lang: The conclusion is scarcely to be avoided. Christianity in a certain sense failed in its purpose of reforming the human race.

But does this failure illustrate the idea that contingency runs right through the universe; that even such an operation as launching the spiritual impulse of an evolutionary period can be subject to accident? There is another possibility—that failure was in some way *intended*. Was the partial failure of Christianity sanctioned by the higher powers to achieve a purpose which could not be achieved in any other way?

I found one very powerful fragment embedded in a letter from T.P. He was referring to a benign intervention which had been made in the everyday life of someone he knows and in it he referred to the occasional necessity for failure as an integral part of the evolutionary process.

Quite simply he mentioned his belief that *failure may have a place on a cosmic scale no less than in the affairs of the human race.*

This is an extract:

W.T.P. Yes, of course I intervened, since when I have been waiting for the response. The art of such intervention consists in a process of not infringing any Karmic barriers, a lesson it takes a long time to master ... On the success or failure of any particular spiritual exercise we should be careful to distinguish between the Christos and the channels through which its energies flow. The Christos is responsible for providing the energy and the inspiring incentive but the Christos is not responsible for choosing the channels. These are chosen by what might be called the Elder Brothers of the human race. *Sometimes they deliberately sanction what we call failure for reasons well beyond our present ken.* There are certain seeds of success which can only germinate in the womb of what we call failure and this is true both cosmically and in relation to our individual lives.

Part Two

CHAPTER SIX

Some Links

Lang: What now follows is a series of scripts by T.P. not apparently connected to the chief focus of his interest in the last five years, namely the historical glimpses of Jesus.

Though they may seem at first glance to be far removed from his main theme, they have been produced for inclusion in this book and it is to be presumed that they are relevant to a purpose of which, perhaps, the Jesus glimpses form only a part.

It may also be that the reader will find relevance and make connections in proportion to his own degree of understanding.

In the case of the three scripts where specific historical periods are involved, the reader will no doubt speculate on the possibility that such periods are related by some personal connection with T.P. himself.

This is not a speculation for which any evidence can be expected but it is a speculation which I have some reason to believe is warranted.

The first script "The Archangelic Hierarchy" is based on a recent talk to a private group and perhaps for this reason he has added some explanatory material designed to amplify it for general readership. It very clearly illustrates the heights to which his seership can reach and is perhaps more specific than the material which he is usually prepared to make available for open readership.

The last script, "And With No Language But a Cry", reveals in remarkably unguarded language his personal participation in noumenal events at the present time.

I can only say that the "conference" described now towards the close of his life matches a similar event in 1917 in Palestine and a second similar "meeting" in the early days of the second world war. The Silent Minute movement was in fact endorsed on this second occasion and I think we are entitled to conjecture that the third event now revealed will initiate a further act of co-operation with higher intention.

There is some reason to believe that on the second occasion, which took place in December 1939 certain assurances were given which resulted in the raising of a cone of protection over these islands. There is also a hint that the conflict was shortened by two years. The only comment I can extract from T.P. about these matters is this. "The complete story of why invasion never took place has not yet been told. You can certainly say that it involved an element of the miraculous."

In 1939 we were plunged into a struggle which to almost all of those involved seemed entirely material, military and national. In hindsight it is now seen to have involved forces and powers on an enormously greater scale. Some sort of hidden alliance existed—perhaps there were several such—and the devoted service of a few provided the fulcrum on which massive assistance from higher levels could be exercised.

Today we are faced with a crisis on a still greater scale.

SOME LINKS

Again contact has been established between mundane and supra-mundane levels. Could it be that we are now offered the chance once again to alter causality, to invalidate "prophecy" and to influence the outcome of the Armageddon "now raging in the Spheres and in the hearts and minds of men"?

CHAPTER SEVEN

The Archangelic Hierarchy

W.T.P. In attempting to deal with certain events now taking place in regions beyond our ken it should be remembered that there are no words in human language capable of describing such events adequately, if at all. What follows therefore should be looked upon as belonging to the realm of symbolism and allegory rather than as embodying factual statements. By "factual" I mean statements capable of proof through the use of reason within the confines of the three dimensional conditions now surrounding us.

Angels and Archangels are not highly evolved human beings, but belong to a different order of creation. They do not incarnate in a material sense on any of the planets in our solar system, which are believed to contain life and intelligence clothed in form.

For this reason, we cannot grasp or understand in full either the appearance of these great Beings, or the role they play in the divine drama of Creation. What follows, therefore, should be regarded as a fragmentary and very partial account of this immensely important hierarchal Order.

Firstly, and to clear the air, let it be said that we humans, no matter how advanced our spiritual status may become, are never transformed or translated into "Angels" or "Archangels". Our progress and development continue

THE ARCHANGELIC HIERARCHY

into eternity, whereas Archangels and their Hosts belong to an order of perfection which although by no means static, does not involve what we understand by the word "evolution".

Also it should be remembered that Nature Spirits and the Intelligences who direct, and control the rhythmic impulses within the Kingdoms of Nature are not "Angels". They belong to an Order of their own which is subject to its own laws of being and progression.

We are dimly aware, mainly through tradition, of the existence of seven Archangels, operating within our solar system. It appears that for periods of unknown duration and controlled by cosmic rotation, each of the seven takes precedence in responsibility for the general oversight of one planet at a time under the guidance of the Solar Deity.

Archangels rule over their own "Hosts of Angels", the number of whom we are unable to compute. Their main function is to infuse into all life processes operating within every realm of being within our system, certain specific "Light" radiations. These radiations so far as can be discerned, emanate from seven Mother or Master Rays.

Each of these Rays embodies (in the main) a specific quality or attribute. These might be summed up in a general way under the headings: Wisdom, Love (the two major Rays now in process of blending), Seership, Beauty, Intuition, Joy and Incentive. We are now in deep water, because our concepts of the meaning of these words vary so widely. For this reason it is perhaps unwise to use words for the purpose of describing the qualities and functions of these Rays.

There is never ceasing interplay between these seven

Rays and those who direct their activity, intensity, range and operation.

There is little we can know for certain about these matters and in fact much of what we think we know is little more than speculation.

What we feel we can accept as accurate is the belief that we are now entering a new chapter in human history; and that it is the Archangel Michael whose turn it is to be associated most closely with our planet and with all forms of life upon it. Biblical and esoteric tradition can, I think, throw some light upon this Archangel's significance and status. There is a chapter in *Michael: Prince of Heaven** containing a list of the titles and qualities traditionally associated with this Archangel. Here are some of them:

1. "Who is like unto the Countenance of God."
2. Recorder of the deeds of men in the heavenly books.
3. The Celestial medium through whom the Law was given.
4. Captain of the heavenly Hosts.
5. Slayer of the dragon of evil intention.
6. Guardian of the holy Sanctuaries.
7. Preparer of the Way before each Messenger from God.
8. Leader of the Church triumphant in Heaven and militant on earth.

What interests us most is the age-old conception of Michael as the Standard Bearer for the Christ and the Preparer of the Way before the advent of God's Messengers to man. It is in the above capacities that he and his mission

* Published by the Chalice Well Press, Glastonbury, Somerset.

should be considered of special importance to us at present.

The use of modern terms to describe Michael's principal task may not be out of place. He is the chief engineer in charge of the sluice gates which control and regulate the release of the "Waters of the Spirit" into our midst. The reservoirs behind these gates contain infinite supplies, capable of serving human needs far into the future.

Use here could be made of an analogy. Man employs the movement and the pressure of water in order to generate electricity. Michael and his co-workers use a similar process for converting the "Waters of the Spirit" into rays and radiations. The latter are stepped down to a point where they can enter safely into the minds and the lives of all forms of sentient and non-sentient life on earth. This stepping down process is regulated in such a way as to meet our present and progressive needs. Such a task is beyond our power to visualise but it is as well that we should be aware, however dimly, that it is going on.

The first effect of a speeding up of these processes is to shake the earth to its foundations, in the form of wars, tribulations, racial disturbances and seismic upheavals. It is true that our world has never been free from these conditions, but when they become so widespread as they are now, we can know that the end of an Age and the birth of a new one are on our doorstep.

In a metaphysical sense, what I have been describing as seemingly outward events is also taking place within you and me. We cannot escape from the battlefield, which means that our thoughts, prayers, words and deeds can all prove useful—or the reverse—to Christ's Standard Bearer.

THE ARCHANGELIC HIERARCHY

The ways in which we co-operate can only be decided individually but the value of collective and individual prayer and meditation is immense and in these ways we can certainly serve Michael and all who are co-operating with him.

There is also another method through which we can make our influence felt. All over the world there are islands, springs, hills and sanctuaries that have been long associated with the name of Michael. Let beacons be lighted upon them either in thought, in actual deed, or in both. Geographical centres of this kind can and do play their part in the general plan now coming into active being.

During the next three centuries, in fact from the present time onwards, Michael and his colleagues have been entrusted with a special task. This is to bring down to human levels a better understanding of the meaning and importance of beauty. This word could be interpreted as the blending of thought, sound, sight and feeling into a condition of harmonious accord with one another. There is good reason why we should co-operate according to our several abilities in helping to further this great purpose.

It is probable that this Michael Age of ours will be given until around A.D. 3500 in which to fulfil itself, although as the texture of "Time" is subject to change, so are human measurements of it.

Michael directs his mission from his own solar dwelling places. As Leader of the Archangelic Host, in a certain sense he combines within himself the qualities of his colleagues as well as his own.

Although not a member of the Archangelic Order, the being known to us as Zoroaster has an important part to play in these cosmic ventures.

Lang: In any attempt to discuss the Michael impulse now entering human consciousness it is inevitable that seeming contradictions will arise in trying to describe an interplay of action between a four dimensional state and our present three dimensional condition.

W.T.P. We have spoken about the increase in human enlightenment that will result from the acceptance by Man of this new impulse, and as a result the impression is inevitably given that the essence of this new enlightenment is contained within the impulse itself. This is not the case. The wave of cosmic energy is in itself neutral—that is to say, although it emanates from a celestial source, its content in the human sense is neither "good" nor "bad". Pure Energy of this kind does not conform in its action to human codes of morality or to our conceptions of "good" and "evil".

All the illumination, knowledge, enlightenment needed for human evolution during the present Round, is *already* embedded within human consciousness, in essence and in embryo. It always has been so because it is an integral part of the creative act.

This new wave of energy will not bring with it the enlightenment so sorely needed at the present time. The potency it contains will, however, be capable of awakening within man the vision and the knowledge which he requires. This is *already* part of his heritage and his very make up, lying secretly and in embryo in the sanctuary of his soul. Thus the wave of energy is an awakener and not an originator of something Man already owns.

The measure of freewill we possess leaves Man in a position to use rightly, or to misuse, the knowledge of spiritual verities, as this unfolds within him.

CHAPTER EIGHT

The Michael Tor, Glastonbury

W.T.P. My findings so far are scrappy and incomplete. And no wonder that this is so, for this mount was already a cosmic centre in pre-Atlantean days.

There are certain places around our planet which owe their formation and destiny to heavenly influences and this is one of them. This means that they still possess a direct link with the energies emanating from the Archangelic Hierarchy, and in the case of the Avalon Tor, with Michael in particular.

The "markings" on the ground of a giant Zodiac around Avalon—a symbolic replica of planetary constellations—now remain the only external link with celestial Agencies.

Within a thousand years or so of man emerging from the animal state and becoming a human individual, the Tor became one of the many global centres where the worship of the Sun, representing its spiritual origin, Light, was practised, Light being the source of all manifestations of life and being.

The Fatherhood of the Creator was the central theme in those very ancient days when both the mount itself and the spring at its foot were enveloped in a sacred aura of protection. Later, much later, when a change in dispensation came about, an interregnum occurred. During this the whole planet passed through a period of catastrophes, earthquakes and violent seismic disturbances. Many areas of the globe became oceans where land had previously stood and vice versa. Avalon Tor, although shaken and deprived of the forests which clothed it, remained an upright land mark and a beacon for seafarers.

Much later came a period during which pre-Osiric influence held sway. Divine Motherhood replaced Fatherhood as the keynote of worship, with the moon as the focus of veneration. The "Intention" appears to have been that this epoch should be followed by the merging of the Sun/Moon eras into a period during which the Father/Mother conception of creation should become the central theme. Something went wrong. Was this perhaps the event that has come down to us as the legend of the Fall? Dark magic, sex as a sensual battling ground replaced the purity of all previous spiritual exercises and the sacred aura of protection was withdrawn.

Meanwhile the Atlantean and Lemurian cataclysms had come and gone, bringing entirely new aspects to the evolutionary life processes on our planet. Time passed during which only the hidden *seed* of the cosmic energies surrounding such centres as this Tor, survived. There followed a period of wilderness in and about the Tor and even a sense of utter desolation. The sun appeared to be darkened in the heavens and the moon cast a disturbing glow in its place. The seemingly sinister effects of the "Fall" became only too apparent in the lives of men.

Much later, worship of Divinity was replaced by the worship of external nature. This involved reverence for the elements, the building of temples to the trees and belief in springs as the symbolic source of life and being. Time rolled on and on until a pre-Druid race emerged

THE MICHAEL TOR, GLASTONBURY

through whose activities nature worship began to be co-related to belief in the Spirit of the Spheres and when Religion came to the forefront once more.

Much later, groups of men (and women) more highly evolved than the "savages" began to isolate themselves at certain strategic points all over the planet, inspired by the conception of a central Unity, the Overlord of all the Gods.

The time had now come when, if life on this earth was to be preserved, Initiates from celestial realms were obliged to descend into incarnation; and in due course their leavening presence helped to prevent this planet from becoming a lifeless moon before its time. One or more of these Initiates took bodily form within the ranks of the Druidic "priesthood", and sacred centres such as our Tor began to be relighted. Preparations were made for the reception of a "Saviour", who would embody the Christos principle on earth. The Tor became an observatory, a centre for the study of the stellar spheres, a place where rituals and rites converged upon the conception of *Oneness* throughout the Universe, seen and unseen.

Terraces still remain around the slopes of the Tor which may well conceal labyrinthian passages beneath. Aspirants for Initiation who found their way through and up this maze emerged at the summit for illumination, but *many* fell by the way.

There was what one might call a "Turning in the Heavens" and this began to be reflected here and there on earth.

Cosmic revelation was at hand.

Then, as was to be expected, the forces of the Left mounted an attempt to obstruct evolution and to bring devolution into action once more. One result, so far as the Druid dispensation was concerned, was the transformation of spiritual practices into a debased form of ritualism from which the spirit had departed. However, I am convinced that a pure strain of Druidic lore persisted at Avalon, thereby creating the right conditions for the arrival of Joseph of Arimathea and his fellow pilgrims, bringing with them the Message of the Christ.

Following nearly 2,000 years of the era known as "Christendom", the time is now come when such centres as the Michael Tor and Chalice Well will emerge into the daylight once more and thereby fulfil a destiny prescribed for them from the birth of time, and to the Glory of God.

CHAPTER NINE

The Closing Days of Atlantis

W.T.P. Wars had developed between the people of the Northern lands (or Islands) and the people of the South.

There had always been friendly competition in achievement between the inhabitants of these two Atlantean areas, and much friction that might have come about was avoided by the fact that a fairly wide strip of ocean divided the series of islands in the South from those belonging to the Northern group.

The latter were in closer touch with the mainlands (the continent of Africa) where human and animal life at that period in history was far lower in evolution and intelligence than those present in the Atlantean civilisation.

A Council of State ruled both the Northern and the Southern lands, and its President was chosen from among its members once in every nine year period. The Council itself was what might be termed a religious/scientific body, that is to say that its members were experts in the practice of religious and esoteric rites and ceremonies, and also were pioneers in scientific and astropsychical research.

Usually, the President himself was one who had advanced far along the pathway of esoteric knowledge, and was in touch with the invisible worlds of life and being. (These ideas came to the writer in his dream experience, during which he found himself watching a particular member of the Council, one of those representing the

Southern lands, and with whom the writer felt himself to be identified for the period of the dream.)

A form of revolution gradually developed among the people of the Northern lands, stimulated largely by unwise association with "bad" inhabitants of the mainland, the latter being outside the Atlantean Council's control. Accusations were made against the Council to the effect that its rulings had become autocratic and favoured the people of the Southern lands too extensively. The trouble was smoothed over during several generations but it finally developed into a condition of active conflict. The Council itself (even that august body) became divided within its own organisation, and a minority of its members sided with the Northern group and left the capital (which was on the largest of the Southern islands) in order to join and lead the Northern land's revolt.

The struggle seems to have lasted for many years and to have grown gradually into a bitter and relentless effort to bring about extermination. The Southern group, however, remained the stronger and those who were still members of its Council held deep scientific secrets unknown (in detail) to those who were in control of the Northern lands.

It was apparently at this crucial period in this terrible civil war that researchers attached to the Southern lands Council discovered the means to harness supra-mundane energy through the division of the atom. The substance used for the purpose was not uranium as at present, but was of a fluidic nature.

Once harnessed, a way was devised for concentrating this newly released energy in a dematerialised condition, which could then be transmitted at will by the use of etheric waves, and rematerialised and exploded in any direction or place previously decided upon.

When news of these discoveries was placed before the Council (or all that was left of it), the views of its members were divided as to the wisdom or otherwise of using this terrible new weapon in the conflict still raging with the dissentient Northern islanders.

Time passed . . . and meanwhile the new weapon was perfected and tried out in a small way over the ocean wastes. It proved so successful that the temptation to use it in actual warfare became too strong to be resisted. And so: "To save further useless bloodshed and suffering on both sides", this new weapon, containing derivatives of the universal creative power, was put into operation against the Northern lands to reduce them to submission.

"Success" was almost instantaneous, and the people of the North (or the few that were left) capitulated and sued for peace.

An armistice was arranged, the Council re-formed, and it appeared that a new and better era was in sight.

The new energy was then employed for "peaceful purposes".

Meanwhile, however, strange seismic and magnetic disturbances developed throughout Atlantean areas. Earthquakes, violent storms, seaquakes, great tidal waves, followed one upon another in increasing number and intensity. The Council ordained that all further research work and tests in connection with the harnessing of the new energy should cease and a week of mourning and repentance was decreed in an effort to "restore the balance of Nature's rhythm, which had been upset by the prostitution of power of supernatural origin to bring about destruction and death in human disputes".

Apparently, this measure was introduced too late. In any case, it was without appreciable effect on the events which followed.

The poisonous radio-active current or element projected into the ether and the material atmosphere of Atlantean regions, as the result of the explosive use of the newly released energy, seems to have dislocated the law governing terrestrial magnetism and gravitation. Tidal waves and earthquakes and epidemics continued to grow in violence. Even vast areas of the mainlands were affected by inundations and landslides. Several of the Atlantean islands disappeared beneath the ocean, and the climate surrounding those that remained became dense and humid. The population rapidly declined in numbers. Fear and distress replaced health and happiness.

Finally, it would seem that a greater tidal wave than ever before witnessed, following a tremendous earthquake on and below the bed of the ocean, wiped out what still remained of the great Atlantean civilisation. The people (except for a comparative few who escaped to high ground on the Mainlands) disappeared into the immensities of the inner worlds of life and being.

Let us take heed before it is too late.

CHAPTER TEN

Does History Repeat Itself?

W.T.P. It is useful now and then to consider the extent to which the study of past human history can prove of benefit to us in what we call our "modern world".

That similarities can be traced between events that have happened, often many centuries apart from one another, is an undoubted fact. However, so far as I am aware, no serious study of this phenomenon has yet been undertaken.

It is probable also that truths, often of a cautionary character, are handed down from one generation to another through the symbolical contents of legends, fables, traditions and (so called) fairy stories.

Recently I was looking in to some of the historical and legendary records that have come down to us (often in mutilated form), from the time of the Pharaoh, Akenaton (The Sun God), who reigned in Egypt some 3,500 years ago during the XVIII Dynasty of the Royal Houses of that strange and potent land.

In so far as our historical records extend into the past, it would seem right to infer that Akenaton was the first great Ruler and Prophet known to us, who proclaimed the Oneness of the Creator and the Unity of Mind.

It is still natural for primitive peoples to perceive Gods in Nature and to worship those beings who appear to rule the Elements, as represented by the kingdoms of the air, the waters of the clouds of Heaven, and of the forests and the great animals of the jungle. In Akenaton's time the people of his realm were not primitive in this sense, yet the multiplicity of the Gods they worshipped had already passed beyond the bounds of reason. It is evident that the priestly class (a very tight and powerful clan) encouraged and promoted the veneration and worship of life through the creation of myths which depended for their existence on belief in innumerable Gods, and also in the divine attributes of the Pharaohs, as traced back and back, from Dynasty to Dynasty, into the mists of time.

Akenaton set himself the herculean task of breaking this tradition.

He proclaimed the Unity of the one God, a God of Light, whose symbol was the Sun. In his time the priestly clan had become corrupt, and true religion had departed from the land.

We know very few details of the struggle through which Akenaton set himself to break the stranglehold of the priests over the common people, and even over those who were cultured and belonged to the aristocracy. What a formidable battle he must have waged!

He himself was delicate from birth, the result, no doubt, of centuries of inbreeding. It is believed that he was subject throughout his short life to epileptic fits. Yet his energy and vision were remarkable. Temporariliy he won his fight against the priests and curbed their power, and cleansed the temples of much vice, ignorance and corruption.

The supreme Creator of the Universe became the ONE GOD to whom, through the Light of the Sun, all eyes and hearts and minds must be directed.

What an achievement this was indeed!

DOES HISTORY REPEAT ITSELF?

His whole life was spent in countering intrigues against his person and his rule. No wonder that he had little time to devote to foreign affairs, with the result that his empire shrank and his generals suffered many defeats both within the state and in foreign lands as well. Akenaton's great legacy to destiny and to the future was in the propagation of one Idea, the unity and omnipotence of the Godhead. Even though, following his tragic death, the priests regained control and the worship of many gods returned, nothing could altogether obliterate the immense value of the seed that he had sown.

The popularity of Akenaton among the common people, the fellaheen, was said to have been remarkable. He was approachable in a way that no previous Pharaoh had ever been. Also, he was credited with possession of the "healing touch", both in regard to diseases and to sin.

This royal and hereditary prerogative is said to have been also owned by the English Plantagenet and Tudor Kings and to be traceable back to King David himself. Doubtless this gift is still in the possession of our royal line. Perhaps it will be brought into use again some day?

History does not tell us clearly how Akenaton met his earthly end. My own belief is that he was murdered at the instigation of the High Priest of Upper Egypt whom he had removed from power and office. A nest of scorpions was inserted beneath the pillows of his couch and his death came slowly but surely, following this dastardly act of evil.

It is no doubt true that history never repeats itself in quite the same way. Jesus the Christ was not the ruler of an earthly empire, although he came, in a hereditary and bodily sense, of a royal line of leaders and of prophets.

DOES HISTORY REPEAT ITSELF?

He came to proclaim the ONE GOD, the Father of all men, and his Father, too. He met the fury of the priests, far more deadly than the anger of the Roman rulers of the time.

He attempted to cleanse the Temple and to bring the true spirit back into religion. And he met his earthly end through the malice of the priestly class who, humanly speaking, were not aliens but of the same Hebrew stock as himself.

What steps can be taken now and in our own age for preventing the repetition of history, as outlined by the earthly fate both of Akenaton and of Jesus? As we look around, are we so certain that the fate of the next Messenger from God will not be similar? During the Christian dispensation is it not true to say that more wars and cruelties have been inflicted in the name of religion, than from any other single cause?

Can humanity at long last begin to learn and profit from the lessons of the religious history of past ages? If so, there is hope for the destiny and welfare of those who are to follow us. Otherwise there can be little.

In comparing the fate of Jesus with that of Akenaton, it must not be thought that I presume to place them on the same spiritual level, or, in fact, to suggest that these two beings were "equal" or to be regarded from the same stance. Let this be made very clear; having said this, let us seek to learn the important lesson that can come from a study of how human history can repeat itself, even if such repetitions are never completely identical, either in procedure or in outcome.

CHAPTER ELEVEN

Prophecy in Relation to the Day of the Lord

There are a number of modern students of Biblical prophecy who interpret the scriptures, both the New and the Old Testament in an exclusively literal way. In considering the relation of current human events to the period known as the "Latter Days" great care should be taken, I think, to try to interpret prophecy in a symbolical and a spiritual sense rather than in an entirely literal manner.

In order to illustrate what I mean, consider certain prophecies about the "Day of the Lord" which have come down to us from early times. Before doing so it is well to remember that religious writers using Oriental tongues were in the habit of expressing themselves in language filled with picturesque and symbolic phraseology.

When such writings are translated into our prosaic English, the literal translations resulting can prove misleading, especially if they are regarded as embodying descriptions of actual historical events due to happen in future times.

As an example let us take one of the most remarkable utterances in the New Testament as recorded in the second Epistle of St. Peter, chapter iii, verse 10:

"But the day of the Lord will come as a thief in the

night; in the which the heavens shall pass away with a great noise, and the elements shall melt with fervent heat, the earth also and the works that are therein shall be burned up."

Here it is stated that the Day of the Lord, elsewhere referred to as the Second Coming will arrive as "a thief in the night", a strange phrase indeed in such a context. Evidently the writer's intention was to make it clear that the event in question is to come both suddenly and unexpectedly. Further, we can reasonably infer that this Coming will manifest itself in a totally unlooked for *manner and form*.

It is not at all clear from the context, for instance, that the Lord whose "Day" it is to be, will appear in a human body and in one place at a time, or in some other manner altogether.

We will return to this when referring to another prophecy; but meanwhile there is the rest of this extraordinary text to be considered. "In the which" (or during which) Coming, both the heavens and the earth are to disappear amid noise, tumult and fire. If we take this sinister forecast literally, then the Day of the Lord would apparently end in a vacuum, all forms of life on earth having ceased to exist.

Here we are faced by an enigma which is seemingly impossible to unravel.

Can the words "Heaven" and "Earth" be regarded as symbols and not as tangible realities? Some commentators interpret the terms "Heaven" and "Earth" as used in prophecies of this kind, not as celestial and terrestrial abodes but as states or conditions of consciousness. It is conceivable that the appearance of a spiritual leaven within the mind of man could result in such a transformation of human consciousness as to bring about a "passing away" of the old methods of thought altogether, to be replaced by something entirely new. Such an event would naturally cause so much confusion and alarm as to create a "great noise", speaking symbolically.

We are next told that following or during this disappearance or transformation "the elements shall melt with a fervent heat". Taken literally this is not a bad description of what happens during an atomic explosion. But in the above context the word "elements" probably refers to climate and atmospheric conditions around the earth. "Fervent heat" could be interpreted as a purifying agent.

The physicist will not allow any connection to be made between mind and matter where the elements of nature are concerned. The metaphysician, however, would take another view. He would sanction the possibility that one result of the transformation of human consciousness could well be that a similar phenomenon would take place in climatic and atmospheric conditions, the elements of which would also be transformed and purified to conform with the change in humanity's mental outlook.

Such a line of reasoning may seem far-fetched and an unlikely solution of the problem. I have set down these suggestions solely for the purpose of turning thought away from dwelling too exclusively on the literal interpretation of the Scriptures in respect of prophecy.

In St. Matthew's Gospel (ch. xxiv, v. 27), Jesus is reported as having used words which have come down to us in the following English form:

For as the lightning cometh out of the east, and shineth even unto the west; so shall also the coming of the Son of man be.

Lightning is a form of very rapid illumination. The implication of this text may well be that the signal for the Coming we are to expect in the Latter Days of our Age will be either preceded or accompanied by a flash of spiritual illumination or understanding which will shine right across the horizons of human consciousness "from East to West" (i.e. from end to end). We should be wrong, I think, to picture this event as if it referred to a metereological phenomenon in the skies above our heads.

Jesus makes it very clear that the Coming is not to be looked for in any one place, i.e. in the desert or in the secret chamber (v. 26) but that it will be universal in its manifestation. This seems to rule out the advent of a Divine Person in human form at any one place. In fact, the "Son of Man" as here used, evidently refers to the coming of an Illumination capable of transforming the minds and hearts of men throughout the world. Such an interpretation does not invalidate the possibility, perhaps the certainty, that a Messenger or Messengers from God may incarnate in our midst in these Latter Days for the purpose of "fulfilling the law and the prophets".

When the great awakening or transformation takes place then it will be possible to realise and recognise universally the Presence of the Christ in the very midst of human consciousness, the complete culmination of the Coming we are told to hope for, prepare for and expect.

St. Paul, in the Second Epistle of Timothy (ch. iii, v. 1),

speaks of the perilous times that shall come in the "last days", but here he may be referring exclusively to the last days on earth of those to whom he was then writing.

According to the words attributed by St. Matthew to Our Lord (ch. xxiv, v. 29–31) the "Sign of the Son of Man" shall appear in heaven (in consciousness) immediately after the tribulations of those days. This event is to be preceded by the darkening of the sun, moon and stars, which could well symbolise the almost universal materialism rampant at that time within the whole firmament of man's mind, belief and action. (In other words the "darkening of the Spirit" by which we are surrounded almost universally at present.)

I have taken these Biblical quotations more or less at random for the purpose of seeing to what extent it is reasonable to interpret prophecies connected with the Latter Days in ways that make some sense to our present understanding. The interpretations I have given may not lead us to any definite or final conclusions concerning these great mysteries. They are set down as food for thought, in order that the reader may carry forward the line of research I have indicated, and so be able to form his own conclusions.

Whatever may be in store for the human race we can rest assured that the Divine Laws of Love, Justice and Grace (Mercy) WILL be fulfilled both now and throughout Eternity.

CHAPTER TWELVE

Chivalry

W.T.P. I was once asked to talk to the pupils of a co-educational school on the subject of chivalry and was sitting in my study gathering my thoughts when I heard a knock on the door, and an old man walked in whom I had never seen before. He was not much to look at but his eyes were kind and his long white beard flowed down over the cloak he was wearing and it shone like a silver stream in the moonlight. He looked as if he had lived a very long time and he gave me the impression of being a pilgrim who had come from a great distance and had travelled in more worlds than one. He clearly understood my thoughts and said: "If you will have a little patience I will give you a few ideas that may prove helpful.

"Simply stated, to be chivalrous is to serve gallantly and cheerfully those around you who are in need of help and to do this without thought of recompense.

"Each thought a person thinks releases energy of some kind and this goes out in ever widening circles of activity and influence. Some such thoughts become translated into deeds and so fulfil their mission for good or ill in your outer world. The majority of thoughts, however, remain unexpressed in action but their influence remains none the less.

"A thought is a vibration and to men of vision every sincere and good thought can be seen as a ray of light and

CHIVALRY

colour flowing out from the thinker very much in the way a wireless wave radiates from a transmitter.

"Every thought you think is pooled and passes into a reservoir which, being fed by each human mind, becomes a latent or active influence for good—or the reverse.

"Everyone who fills his mind with thoughts of love and hope and the will to serve becomes a torch bearer and sends forth invisible rays of light and healing. On the other hand every thought of anger, fear and selfishness adds to the darkness and fog which have spread so dangerously around your planet.

"A mind that is filled with peace and the will to good is like a beacon set on a hill, which spreads its radiance far and wide and helps to light up the dark places in human consciousness far beyond the immediate neighbourhood of the thinker. 'Let your light so shine before men . . .' said the great Master. He was referring to the light of the mind and the spirit before which no darkness can prevail for long.

"There is another form of chivalry which is near to my heart. It is the chivalry which consists of sparing a thought for the Lord of your planet. He is responsible for controlling life and action in the mineral and vegetable kingdoms. The spirit of all natural things is under his direction, the spirits of the trees and flowers of the mountains and the valleys, the grass, the rivers and the seas and all that grows both above and beneath the ground. Where I have come from the Lord of the Planet is known as Sanyat Kumara. You may know him as The Ancient of Days. Think what difficulties he is enduring at the present time!

CHIVALRY

"The hand of man is bringing tragedy and chaos to the world of nature by tearing minerals out of the ground and turning them into engines of war with which to destroy not only human life but all that is fair and beautiful on your planet. Trees are uprooted and the gifts of nature intended for the welfare of mankind are being converted into implements of death or devastation and rendered worse than useless.

"The sounds of explosions which rock the earth spread terror among the 'little people' who live upon the ground and beneath it and who inhabit the trees and rivers and the air above your heads.

"If men continue wilfully to misuse these natural gifts in such a tragic way you must not be surprised if the green fields and forests become deserts of sand and desolation and if springs and rivers dry up, if the oceans invade the land and the earth quakes beneath your feet.

"When you pray to God ask that you may be used to help in spreading the Light of His Love so that the darkness of ignorance and sin may disappear. And in your prayers, remember the Lord of the Planet and all who work under him in the kingdoms of nature. Ask that man may be forgiven for the wrong he is doing to the 'little people' for whom I plead. They wish to be your friends and helpers and deserve better treatment at your hands than they are receiving. Be chivalrous towards them in your thoughts and actions, for they are helpless to defend themselves against the evil that men do.

"However, let there be no fear in your hearts, because victory of light over darkness is assured. Remember the great Master who said: 'I am the Light of the World.' Follow in his footsteps and learn to draw upon his light so that you may become torchbearers in his service. Remember also that you are surrounded by invisible hosts of those who are also in his service and who work under the inspiration of the one infinite MIND.

"Their thoughts and prayers are with you."

My visitor then said goodbye and went away.

CHAPTER THIRTEEN

Questionnaire

Lang: T.P. insists that his purpose at the present time is to release certain insights into ultimate questions for the ordinary reader "whilst leaving occultists to fend for themselves". The deciding factor appears to be whether the information has a practical, daily-life application or not. It is, indeed, impossible to read much of this material without being influenced in a practical everyday sense and where this effect is obtained, it meets, I would guess, his intentions.

Yet there is a whole area of T.P.'s material which appears to be theoretical in the highest degree; the Archangelic Hierarchy is one example.

There is in most of us a hunger to be told about the worlds we believe to exist but which we lack the spiritual organs to investigate for ourselves. Some such hunger was regarded by Gurdjieff as one of the cosmic "sacred impulses" which he defined as "the desire to know ever more about the laws of world-creation and world-maintenance". Mere curiosity was not, however, to be confused with this cosmic striving and the merely curious were subjected to devastating strictures.

For those of us who find it very difficult indeed to distinguish between a divine impulse and a personality hunger feeding on vanity, the only course would seem to

QUESTIONNAIRE

be to blunder on asking our questions and being slapped down when necessary.

With something of this in mind I put a number of "ultimate" questions to T.P. Some he did not answer at all. A few he answered as though I had asked something quite different. A number he answered quite straightforwardly.

In the belief that the average reader of this book will have a roughly similar distillation of ultimate questions hovering somewhere at the back of his mind, I have included a few of my questions and T.P.'s replies. Here they are.

Lang: Is there a Divinity that oversees us?

W.T.P. If by "Divinity" is meant the first Cause, the primary Source of Creation and Life, the Supreme Mind, then use of the word "oversees" in its literal sense is inapplicable. If this word is replaced by the term "awareness", then the answer would be YES. There is no kind or form of life which does not contain within itself, to a lesser or greater extent, an infusion of the infinite Mind to which it owes its existence. What we mean by "overseeing" is embodied in the operation of primary law instituted by the First Cause in an act promulgated before life became embodied in form.

My use of the word form includes qualities and attributes which cannot be described in words.

We do not know the mechanics or the methods by which Cosmic Law is administered.

We can only guess at the way in which Divine Agencies, Archangels, Hierarchies, Solar and Planetary "Rulers" were conceived and constituted almost certainly long before other forms of life (including the human species) emerged.

It can be said that in the administration of primary law the Being who rules our planet and its interior counterparts does exercise "oversight" as well as awareness but he does this in a sense which cannot be described in words. If the Universe is governed by inviolate Law, how do we account for the seeming lawlessness which to human sense surrounds us on every side? In what way can lawlessness serve the requirements of primary Law? Here we are beyond our depth, partly because we know so little about that portion of Law dealing with cause and effect. Nevertheless, we can surmise that Law is the ultimate master even within the illusory conditions of life in which we now find ourselves.

It is far beyond the comprehension of the human mind as at present constituted to grasp what we call Absolute Truth. For instance, we refer to the assertion that "God is Love" as an absolute truth, but as we are unable to conceive what the concepts "God" or "Love" embrace and signify from the standpoint of pure reality, our speculations are thus confined within the limitations of a series of relative truths, half truths and incorrect conceptions of what "Truth" actually is.

The human mind as at present constituted is capable only of surveying and pursuing relative truths, whereas one would need to stand at the point of absolute truth before being able to analyse and value the qualities of the myriad lesser "truths" set out in theology, occultism and the rest.

We possess no concrete standard at present which would give us the capacity to disentangle the countless forms of relative truth and then discard them one by one till they all disappear in the ocean of Truth itself.

The approach of the mystic is to base his whole outlook and with unshakeable faith on the primary concept of what we dimly perceive as "goodness" based on law, this law being infused with the qualities of omnipotence, omniscience and omnipresence. If one tries to start from any other foundation (however theoretical the above basis may seem to be to finite understanding) then one can wander endlessly in and out of the maze of relative truths without any satisfaction and without getting anywhere worth while.

It is the "child" who gets into the Kingdom of Heaven and all the wisdom of the intellectuals and the occultists is incapable in itself of rising out of relativity into "light".

Anything I write, for instance, is subject inevitably to "relative" considerations. What has been suggested as the principal function of our planetary Ruler in relation to Law can be said to apply in a far wider and more comprehensive sense to the cosmic Being in charge of the solar system to which we belong. Any attempt to "look up further" leads only to frustration. In my view the surmise is fully warranted which implies that Life, both individualised and in embryo manifesting *throughout* our solar system is linked in its unfoldment and is interdependent in its progress and ultimate purpose.

My thesis is that the First Cause, having established Law

to govern all Creation, does not thereafter interfere or intervene in its operations. Awareness but not "oversight" exercised through the Law, can be ascribed to "Deity", but here again, such a statement can only express a speculative point of view.

Lang: Is mankind older than science thinks?

W.T.P. My own belief is that races of men have inhabited this planet for a far longer period than can be assessed by the discoveries of fossils and similar traces of human habitation here. The original human species completed their cycles of existence on earth level many millions of years ago, so far distant from us in "Time" that all external traces of their presence have been obliterated, even in fossilised or any other material form.

Lang: What is the real constitution of Man?

W.T.P. This cannot be defined in words. Is the question intended to be confined to the particular section of the race who are in process of incarnating and reincarnating during the current Round of Evolution? Occultists speak of each of these Rounds lasting for about 25,000 years of terrestrial time but I would hesitate to place this limit on the duration of a single Round. In considering the constitution of Man it would be unwise to rule out the group soul thesis as applied to a considerable portion of the human species now among us. However, in my view such a thesis does not indicate that the seeds, the potential of individual identity *are* present in every unit within the group soul formation, even if to a very embryonic degree.

We speak of "man" possessing a body, a soul, a mind and a spirit. These are only words and give no clear idea what man actually really is. To say that man is a spirit tells us little for if we knew what spirit is we should know what Deity is, and we do not possess this knowledge. All one can hazard is that man, having emerged from group soul limitations, is in himself an "I Am", an individualised expression of life, who possesses intelligence, perception, incentive and feeling.

This I AM is clothed in form, or rather in many forms according to the particular level of his activity, within the seven regions of being he inhabits in sequence.

This sequence is not eternal and in due course gives way to further and unfathomable sequences, of which we know little. Clothing is not the man, although he cannot function without some kind of individualised form, whether living on earth or elsewhere. Complete formlessness belongs to a pre-Creation era about which we cannot even speculate.

The concept expressed by "without beginning or ending" lies outside our comprehension. The physical or any other "body" as indicated above is not the man; but the qualities of mind, intelligence, consciousness, feeling and incentive are his inviolable possessions.

Lang: Was the Incarnation of Jesus an unique event in the whole of human history?

QUESTIONNAIRE

W.T.P. In a certain sense each descent of a Master or Elder Brother into our midst is unique in its own right and in its own time.

One cannot speak of the future but in my view Jesus was the instrument for fulfilling a special act at a particular moment of "time" which had not been attempted in this Round by any of his predecessors.

There is a basic and master rhythm which controls and infuses planetary life energies of every kind and form. One could describe it as creating a central vibratory keynote which vitalises and sustains the continued existence of the primary atom, from which all planetary life, however manifested, is derived, and on which it depends for its existence.

Jesus' central task during his three years Ministry was to act as the medium for "earthing a cosmic 'current' " (for want of a better description) in such a way as to heighten and to speed up the vibratory rate and the rotation of the rythmic processes governing all planetary activities. Jesus spoke of bringing a sword with him and this sword was the instrument he used for carrying out the "earthing" process. He also spoke of bringing "Life" with him—that is, a renewal of our planetary life destined to be ushered in by a change of rhythm. All else was secondary but the successful achievement of his task produced such an overpowering effect upon him, that he was lifted above time and space and "saw" the Coming of the Kingdom on earth as if it were to be an imminent and not a long-term result of what he had been allowed to do. The current of which I speak passed through him and then into his sword and so into the very living soil and structure of the planet. Whether he was fully aware of the process "as a man" we do not know, in the same way that it is uncertain whether he always realised the full import of what was said through him by the Christos.

My surmise is therefore that his accomplishment as I have outlined it was "unique" in method and operation up to the point at which he appeared among us.

Lang: What is the Will of God for Man?

W.T.P. This should be worded differently. The Will of God is concerned with life in all kingdoms and all worlds, mankind being an infinitesimal portion of the whole—certainly not the only portion imbued with intelligence and purpose. The Deific Will is embodied in the primary Law established to supervise and govern life of every kind throughout the millions of universes now in being. It is permissible to suggest that the Will of God could be defined in part as the Divine Intention to express Himself in ways that will ultimately provide Him with a perfect reflection of Himself.

In truth this query concerning the Will of God is unanswerable save by Himself.

Lang: What can a man do to make himself sensitive to higher influences?

W.T.P. Awareness of spiritual realities through unfoldment of man's perceptive faculty is a slow and arduous process. Books and teachers can help him along his way provided that he learns how to *select* and evaluate for himself what books and teachers try to convey. Man's supreme Teacher in this field is to be found in the realm of a complete stilling of the self, a conscious withdrawal into the depths of silence, rejection of every preconceived belief or speculation about the verities or what they are, or from whence derived. We spend about one third of our whole lives in sleep or in a state of comparative quiescence. We can learn more of real value when sleeping than when "awake" providing, by exercise of the prayer of intention, we succeed in rousing the inner self from sleeping too.

Take a single problem or a single query to bed and dwell upon it quietly and without anxiety. Then release it from thought altogether, and pass forward into sleep in the natural way. The response may come on awakening or it may unfold later, but if one's homework has been well done, a response is certain and will prove revealing.

The strong desire to serve from exactly where one stands in spiritual and other attainments will ensure a growing measure of enlightenment and vision, for in service to the Law all things shall be added unto us.

Lang: Can you say anything about the after-death state of the ordinary individual?

W.T.P. I am often asked to try to explain simply how the change called "death" affects the individual. Scriptural teaching on the subject is far too vague to prove of any real service, indeed it can involve a disservice in creating the belief that man goes straight to "Heaven" or to "Hell", according to his deserts, so soon as he departs this life.

I cannot think of any simpler way for dealing with this question than by use of the following symbolism.

On earth we are imprisoned within strong walls. These contain narrow slits through which, by the use of our five senses we can look out on a very restricted scene.

At "death" these walls dissolve as the result of man's entry into a new dimension. Imprisonment is replaced by freedom and the five senses are absorbed into a new and wider form of vision, action and perception.

We take our minds and their associations with us and therefore tend to surround ourselves for a time with "pictures" from the past or with our preconceived ideas about "Heaven" and "Hell".

Gradually the mists disperse, our new faculty of vision and perception comes into play and we begin to realise and enjoy our freedom and to continue our lives quite naturally in the new state of being now surrounding us.

Life goes forward sequentially not in a land of dreams and shadows but in a realm more "solid", more real and far more satisfying than we can ever experience on earth.

We continue to live our own lives both as individuals and in communities, in "town" and "country" as well as within ourselves.

Progress or retrogression, to use our human terms, continues to operate very much in the same way as is the case whilst we are still earthbound.

QUESTIONNAIRE

In due course release from earth conditions brings a sense of freedom and security, never experienced before, which in itself is a joyful foretaste of Heaven. The realisation gradually dawns that Life is encompassed by Love and the pilgrim is able to go forward cheerfully on his destined way with deep thankfulness of spirit, mind and heart.

CHAPTER FOURTEEN

"And With No Language But a Cry"

W.T.P. On being summoned recently to attend a Conference of my superiors, quite an exalted affair in its way, I was asked to outline what I felt to be the needs of the hour, in special relation to the extension of human knowledge. This request took me aback, for in comparison with my questioner's comprehensive knowledge the value of my views and feelings is modest indeed. I asked for the question to be elucidated. Was it intended to refer to any particular section of human activity: religion, politics, social problems, metaphysics? I was told to choose whichever field I felt to be the most important at the present time.

In the rarefied atmosphere which surrounded the occasion, one thinks and "speaks" in a dimension beyond our own. Therefore to translate my response into words of any real meaning is almost impossible. The nearest I can get to clarity is by trying to convey the essence of my central thesis, for what it may be worth. Here it is:

In my view the enlightenment now so urgently needed at human levels has nothing *primarily* to do with man's external life and actions, whether in politics, theology, economics, sociology, or any other similar sphere.

The need is for a spiritual revelation given from an

"AND WITH NO LANGUAGE BUT A CRY"

authoritative source, dealing with those fundamental questions which have remained unanswered satisfactorily, so far as I am aware, during the whole of recorded human history to date. These (I ventured to imply) could be summed up as follows:

Where does man come from and where does he go from here?

What are the conditions and circumstances of his life both before his present birth on this planet and subsequent to his departure?

If it be true that we inhabit earth levels on more than one occasion, both before and after our present existence here, how often does this take place, from the basis of time/space conditions?

How does the Law of Cause and Effect operate as applied to life on our planet as a whole, to nations and to individuals? To what extent are we each responsible for the whole?

If terrestrial events can be foreseen, and as predicted by the prophets of the past events ranging over periods running into thousands of years, are such events "fixed" and unalterable and beyond the influence of human action? If so how does the measure of man's free will which is said to exist, fit into the general plan?

Or in relation to such events is he merely a puppet, a helpless onlooker?

Is the sexual process to remain a permanent ingredient of human evolution?

Does the divine plan involve predestination and pre-determination exercised *solely by the Creator*?

I tried to make it clear that the average man, involved

"AND WITH NO LANGUAGE BUT A CRY"

as he is in the daily struggle for survival, rarely stops to formulate such questions for himself. And that, in any case, the general confusion prevalent and theoretical controversies in the realms of religion and science, leave him bewildered and depressed. I added, however, that, realised consciously or not, man was hungering for enlightenment in the fields of knowledge I have outlined, and without which enlightenment human progress in an upward direction would seem to be impossible. I spoke of the various and conflicting answers given to these questions hitherto by occultists and by leaders of Oriental societies and groups, the total effect of which only added to the general confusion in men's minds. I went further, by giving my considered view that unless authoritative enlightenment of the kind that I had referred to could be provided soon, human progress would be replaced by a period of retrogression and devolution.

The basis of my outbursts could be summarised as follows: "Surely the time has come in the history of the human race when man could be helped to progress more rapidly if provided with enlightenment on the vital and fundamental questions which I have just placed before you?" By this time I was alarmed at my temerity, yet convinced that nothing but common sense underlay my plea. Before I withdrew I was given certain reassurances and a very gracious blessing, but on this occasion answers to my questions were not forthcoming. I realised, of course, that if and when such answers would become available they would proceed from much higher sources than those with whom I had been conferring. Whatever the ultimate outcome may be, it seems to me that the clear and definite *voicing* of our spiritual needs, at this critical moment, may serve a useful purpose, irrespective of the modest status of the questioner.

We are assured that the awaking soul can obtain the spiritual knowledge he requires from the depths of silence within himself and in accordance with his individual needs. This I believe, partly from personal experience, but the call of the hour would seem to warrant the provision of authoritative illumination, sufficiently tangible in expression to reach and be understood by humanity as a whole.

We are surely entitled to insist that our knowledge of Man's destiny and goal should now be extended to meet our present urgencies and to help us to prepare for whatever Fate may hold in store? It has been customary to use the prayer "Lighten our darkness O Lord" as a petition only. The time has come to convert this petition into an imperative call for enlightenment, a call to which we are entitled to receive a speedy response.

To clean the slate every 10,000 years or so may serve a Divine purpose, but as children of Divinity we surely have the right to know at least something of the Father's plans for His family, and how we can co-operate effectively in the carrying out of these plans.

Part Three

CHAPTER FIFTEEN

The Baha'i Faith

Walter Lang Of all T.P.'s glimpses the most touching and poignant for me is the story of the cloak. It is an intensely human story and it bridges not only two thousand years of time but it connects also many levels of a "something" of which time is, perhaps, only a part.

Within this story there is a thread linking not only past and present but linking also a whole continuum of ideas which one can rarely if ever find exemplified in a tangible, everyday aspect. The story was told in *A Man Seen Afar*. In the second year of Jesus' ministry he had gone up into the hills behind Capernaum to rescue a shepherd boy who had lain for several days and nights after breaking a leg. With four others Jesus reached the injured boy, who was now only semi-conscious, but before attending to him in any way, Jesus took off his own cloak and wrapped the injured lad in it.

A miracle then occurred. The rough litter the others had prepared was unnecessary. The boy stood up, quite restored, his broken leg mended and straightened. After arranging for one of those present to stay with the sheep, Jesus blessed the boy and sent him home, still with Jesus' own cloak around his shoulders. At this time the community purse was empty and Joseph of Arimathea was abroad. That night, in bitter winter weather, Jesus was without a cloak.

Mary Magdalene had been given a gold medallion as a keepsake by the Roman officer with whom she was in love and on hearing the story, Mary at once gave the medallion to Judas asking him if he could find a purchaser and with the money, buy Jesus another cloak. In an inn near Capernaum, Judas met the man who appears as "I" in *A Man Seen Afar*. Whether it is permissible to equate this "I" with Tudor Pole or not is a matter that can only be decided by a very careful and intuitive reading of the whole book—and perhaps not even then. For present purposes I refer to him simply as X, it being understood that X was a historical individual alive in Palestine at the time and on the periphery of the Gospel events.

Judas asked X if the medallion was marketable but X informed him that it was not. It was a coin struck for presentation to those receiving the Freedom of the city of Rome and as such it could not under Roman law be sold or bartered. X advised Judas to return the medallion to Mary. He then sent a servant to his Jerusalem home to fetch a nearly new camel-hair cloak which had been given to X by his father as a birthday present. This he gave to Judas, suggesting that Judas should get Mary to alter it as necessary and give it to Jesus. Some time later X saw Jesus and noticed with great pleasure that he was wearing it.

Nineteen hundred years later Tudor Pole, then a major in the British Intelligence Service happened to be walking on Mount Carmel with a very saintly man who is the focus of this present section, Abdu'l Baha Abbas. Noticing that T.P. was shivering in the cold of the late autumn evening, he removed his own camel-hair cloak and put it round T.P.'s shoulders.

At that instant T.P. hears a whisper on the wind which seemed to be saying: "Restitution after many days".

It would be unwise to draw facile conclusions from such a story. But I think it might also be a mistake not to draw any conclusions.

The mechanism which connects our temporal existence with a greater, timeless state is very rarely demonstrated in an evidential way. Yet all of us at one time or another have fleeting, half-remembered subjective experiences which we know with great certainty belong to this category. Very occasionally, however, do we meet an experience told by someone else which we feel intuitively possesses this same "touchstone" validity.

For me this story of a cloak has this. It simply IS. It could not have been invented. It stands outside evidence or argument, yet strangely enough the story is not at odds with logic if seen in terms of many of T.P.'s accounts of what he calls the "*au delà*". He believes that highly-developed souls—whom he refers to as Elder Brothers—are responsible for arranging the genetic vehicle of a Messenger from God. (C. S. Lewis has this same idea and presents it very simply in the dialogue of the Pendragon in *That Hideous Strength*.)

The Ruler of this planet arranges the mission of a Messenger. Then, using a human vehicle moulded by the loving care and perhaps generations-long guidance of the Elder Brothers, the Ruler of the Planet asks the Godhead for the services of the Christos.

The Ruler of the Planet is the channel through whom the Christos flows to overshadow the Messenger.

The Christos is a principle, an emanation of the Godhead. It is not subject to the experiences of the Messenger and it cannot suffer and cannot in any way be subject to the human situation. Thus a Messenger is overshadowed (to a greater or lesser extent) by a divine principle for the period of his mission.

All Messengers are thus suffused with divinity either to the extent of their capacity or to the degree required for their mission. For T.P. this process has never taken place more completely, with a greater surrender or effect than in the case of Jesus. Adherents of some religions might well accept such a thesis while reserving for their own particular revelation the distinction of having the most perfect example. Islam clearly recognises a long series of divine Messengers and accords a very high place to Jesus— a catholicity which Christians appear unable to reciprocate. I would think it unlikely that any ordinary individual is qualified to arbitrate on levels of being so far above his own. What does seem important at the present time is to recognise that the spiritual fertilisation of humanity is a continuous process, utilised time and time again by Messengers from God, and while we may feel that Jesus is the most perfect example of the process, we have surely no right to deny that Deity enters human life at many levels.

To the several millions of adherents of the Baha'i faith, Baha'u'llah, a Persian nobleman who was born in Persia 150 years ago, was a divine prophet and they believe that he was *the* Messenger destined to proclaim the dawn of a new age for the human race. For them, this Founder was the Christ Messenger charged with the task of proclaiming the advent of a religious synthesis on earth.

The Faith which he founded was regarded as heretical by orthodox Muslims and Baha'u'llah and his family were exiled, first to Baghdad, later to Turkey and finally in 1868 to Akka in Palestine where he died in 1892.

For a period of forty years the family existed in conditions of more or less close imprisonment yet, in spite of this fact, the Baha'i Faith continued to spread. It was not until the Young Turks Revolution of 1908 that Abdu'l Baha Abbas, the son of the founder, and his family, were finally freed. They then settled in Haifa. In the local conditions existing towards the close of the First World War, it became apparent that Abdu'l Baha and his family were in great danger. The Turkish Military commander whose H.Q. was between Haifa and Beirut announced that should he be compelled by Allenby's advance to evacuate Haifa, he would crucify the saintly Abdu'l Baha and his entire family on Mount Carmel.

Tudor Pole was able to set in motion certain action which resulted in the lives of Abdu'l Baha and his family being saved. He recounts the details himself in one of the passages which follows.

A relationship of a very intimate kind was established between T.P. and Abdu'l Baha. This has been referred to by T.P. in previous books.

In consideration for the part which Tudor Pole played in those days, and to meet many requests from Baha'i friends, T.P. has included in the present book the scripts which now follow.

CHAPTER SIXTEEN

Personal Recollections of Abdu'l Baha Abbas and the Baha'i Outlook

It was at Constantinople in 1908 that I first heard of a group of Persians, known as Baha'is who were said to be associated with a movement for the promotion of peace and brotherhood among members of all religious faiths. On further enquiry I discovered that their leader, known as Abdu'l Baha (Servant of God), son of the Founder of the Movement, Baha'u'llah, had been a prisoner for nearly forty years and was still confined with his family in the fortress city of Akka in Palestine.

A few months later news was received in London that following the Young Turkish revolution, a general amnesty for religious and political prisoners had been granted and it was in this way that the head of the Baha'i Community regained his freedom.

There can be few alive today who had personal contact with Baha'u'llah, the Founder of the Baha'i Faith; and there can be very few Westerners still alive who knew his son, Abdu'l Baha.

My only link with Baha'u'llah apart from Abdu'l Baha himself was the late Professor Browne, of Cambridge, who has left a record of his meeting in the 1880's with Baha'u'llah, who, after spending many years in Persian and Turkish prisons, died in confinement at Akka in 1892.

PERSONAL RECOLLECTIONS OF ABDU'L BAHA ABBAS

The impression left on Professor Browne was one of surpassing spiritual majesty, accompanied by an aura of holiness leaving no doubt that here one was in the presence of a Messenger from God.

The Coming of Baha'u'llah was heralded by a forerunner known as the Bab (The Gate), who predicted the advent of a Prophet destined to bring fresh illumination to the world. Baha'u'llah was born at Nur in Persia in 1819.

The primary mission of the Baha'i Faith is to enable every follower of earlier world beliefs to obtain a fuller understanding of the religion with which he already stands identified and to acquire a clear apprehension of its purpose. In modern times this will involve the emergence of a worldwide community, a consciousness of universal citizenship and the founding of an international language and culture.

The Baha'i credo is now increasingly demonstrating its right to be recognised not as one more religious system superimposed on the conflicting creeds which have divided mankind for so long, but rather as a restatement of the eternal verities underlying all religions. Its function would seem to be that of a unifying force, instilling into the followers of every Faith a spiritual vigour, infusing them with a new hope and love for mankind, fixing them with a new vision of fundamental unity and unfolding to their eyes the noble destiny that awaits the human race.

The basic principle enunciated by Baha'u'llah is that religious truth is not absolute but relative, that divine revelation is a continuous and progressive process, that all the great Faiths are divine in origin, that their aims and purposes are the same, that their functions are complementary, and that their missions represent successive stages in the evolution of human society.

PERSONAL RECOLLECTIONS OF ABDU'L BAHA ABBAS

Although Abdu'l Baha (who was always known to his family, followers and friends in affectionate reverence as "The Master") would often quote his father's sayings and relate various incidents from his life, he never gave descriptions of his personality, and we are told that the pictures which have come down to us give a very poor impression of his father's stature and dignity.

He wished to be remembered not by his person or his human frame, but by his teachings, and his actions. In this respect, one is sure that Abdu'l Baha, too, would not wish his personality, his physical aspect, to obscure the inspiration of his teachings and the example of his life. I was in close contact with him on many occasions, in Palestine, Egypt, Paris, London and Bristol, and although I retain a clear picture of his gracious and dignified personality, it would not be easy to translate such a picture into adequate words.

The most abiding impression I received from intimate contact with him was his immense breadth of outlook, permeated with the spirit of deep and loving kindness. Whatever the topic under discussion—ranging from religion to the weather, from sunsets to the flowers, from ethics to personal behaviour, Abdu'l Baha always struck the universal note, the note of Oneness as between the Creator and all His creation, great or small.

There is a certain similarity between the origin of the Christian Faith and this modern restatement of the same eternal truths.

As already mentioned, it was the Bab who acted as a John the Baptist in heralding the advent of a great Teacher. He and over 20,000 others were destined to be martyred for their beliefs.

The fundamental truths of life and conduct as proclaimed through Jesus have been reaffirmed in picturesque language by the Baha'i leaders, this reaffirmation being worded to meet the needs of our complex modern "civilisation". The Founders of both these Faiths possessed outstanding powers of healing and seership. Here the comparison ends, for Baha'u'llah was succeeded in his Messianic role by his son, whereas Jesus left no single successor behind him. The ultimate brotherhood of all Mankind, the Oneness of Truth, the spiritual basis behind all Religions, the appeal for the establishment of universal peace—all these are ideals which had been proclaimed by previous Messengers from God.

Like the Quakers, Baha'is renounce the use of force or violence of any kind. So far as I know no attempt was ever made to rescue their leaders from a period of forty years of confinement in Turkish prisons. Baha'is are as pacifist in outlook as the early Christians tried to be.

What is the special appeal voiced by Baha'u'llah and his son, which has resulted in so many of their followers the world over asserting that they are no longer Jews, Christians, Moslems or Buddhists, *as such* but have become Baha'is?

The answer may well be that as each religious revelation becomes crystallised, dogmatic and formal, the need arises for Truth to be restated in terms that conform to the needs of the new hour.

This book so far as been mainly concerned with an attempt to throw fresh light upon the life and times of Jesus as the supreme pioneer and exponent of the Christian ethic. This ethic has never yet been given a fair trial, with the result that we now find ourselves in a dangerous and parlous condition.

To what extent can the Baha'i and other spiritual movements of modern times bring this ethic into practice? It may be of some interest to set down my own fragmentary memories of the daily life and outlook of Abdu'l Baha, as I knew him, and as a man rather than as a Prophet, not with the intention of making a comparison with Jesus, but in the hope of throwing some light upon the ways through which important spiritual movements come into being. Much of the material that follows is fragmentary and may often seem trivial. Trivial incidents in a context of this kind may, however, conceal significant lessons. I should make it clear that, in my view, Jesus' advent in our midst was and is a unique event in world history, an event that is as real and availably present today as it ever was. There can be no question of comparing the status of the various Messengers who from time immemorial have descended among us, each inspired by the Christ principle in his own time and way.

It is from this standpoint that my memories of Abdu'l Baha should be viewed. He was a man of great spiritual stature and prophetic vision and I shall always cherish the affection he bestowed upon me and the inspiration that his life and example have given to me ever since he first came into my life in 1908.

Footnote: In the East the title of "Master" is given to the head of the family or the clan. It is also used to designate the leaders of both secular and religious movements. It is in this sense that I refer to Abdu'l Baha as the Master.

CHAPTER SEVENTEEN

"Ye Are All the Fruits of One Tree, and the Leaves of One Branch"

In the early years of this century the problem of translation was a very difficult one, because no English linguists were available, and the knowledge of English among those of the Master's entourage was scanty to a degree. Only rarely, as I have recorded elsewhere, was I privileged to overcome this problem, when I spoke easily with the Master in a language which surmounted the barriers of the human tongue. I have known times when he realised instinctively that he was being translated incorrectly and then insisted on a fresh interpretation.

There was an occasion in Ramleh when one of his Persian followers was being interviewed by newspaper correspondents. The Master was in the next room but within hearing distance. When asked about his Faith this follower proudly proclaimed that he was a Baha'i and *not* a Christian. Abdu'l Baha came into the room at this juncture and naturally the Press reporters turned their attention to him exclusively. One of them knew Arabic well and was able to glean the substance of the Master's discourse. To the surprise of most present, this consisted of an exposition of the spiritual principles which formed the basis for the teaching of "His Holiness the Christ".

He made it clear that these great principles also formed

"WE ARE ALL THE FRUITS OF ONE TREE"

the foundations for the Message proclaimed by Baha'u'llah, but set forth in a manner most suitable for the needs of humanity in the modern world.

He insisted that his father had come to proclaim anew the unity underlying all religions. He also spoke of the danger of exclusiveness which could only lead to the establishment of a new sect and an abandonment of all that was best and true in Christianity and the ancient world scriptures.

Coffee was then served and to show his friendly tolerance, Abdu'l Baha accepted a cigarette from one of the reporters, allowed it to be lighted, put it to his mouth, and then laid it aside.

Alas, that the full account of this very important occasion has disappeared in the mists of time. Although of a little less than medium height, Abdu'l Baha made an impression on all who met him by his dignity, friendliness, and his aura of spiritual authority. His blue-grey eyes radiated a luminosity of their own and his hands were beautiful in their grace and healing magnetism. Even his movements were infused with a kind of radiance.

His compassion for the aged, for children and the downtrodden knew no bounds. I remember once after he had visited a Salvation Army refuge near the Embankment, in London, tears came to his eyes. He could not understand how a wealthy nation like Britain could allow such poverty and loneliness in its midst. He spoke about this to Archdeacon Wilberforce of Westminster Abbey and to Dr. R. J. Campbell of the City Temple and he provided a sum of money through London's Lord Mayor for the succour of the poor and derelict, then so prominent a feature of the London scene.

"WE ARE ALL THE FRUITS OF ONE TREE"

In speaking to me, he often referred to the need for providing food and sustinence for those in want, as a primary requisite to supplying moral and spiritual food for the heart and for the mind.

The famous declaration that we are all leaves of the same Tree was a constant theme in his conversation. He would dwell in this connection on the example of Jesus, the over-whelming love and understanding of "His Holiness the Christ".

The Master's visit to America left him sad and bewildered. He made it clear to me that the opportunity would be given to our Island and its people to lead the world out of its present darkness into the light of a new day.

At that time, now over half a century ago, it did not seem to me that Abdu'l Baha envisaged the establishment of a new and separate "Religion". All the stress of his teaching was laid on the leavening effect of the Baha'i message on the religions already in existence and which were themselves in such urgent need of spiritual regeneration from within. The Master made it clear that to create an entirely new and separate religious organisation at that time should be resisted vigorously.

It was on this occasion that I presented to the Master gifts from his English friends. I had travelled from Marseilles on a steamer called the *Sphinx* and intended to return overland via. Damascus, Smyrna, Constantinople and Vienna. My return ticket and reservations for the round trip were arranged before I left London. On arrival at Alexandria I lost no time in visiting my revered friend and in carrying out the commission with which I had been entrusted. I speak no Persian and my knowledge of

"WE ARE ALL THE FRUITS OF ONE TREE"

Arabic is rudimentary, and so our conversation was carried on through Abdu'l Baha's grandson, acting as interpreter. At one point the latter was called away, but Abdu'l Baha continued the conversation and I found myself replying! When the interpreter returned, my ability to do so ceased. To make sure that I had understood correctly, I asked for a translation of what Abdu'l Baha had been saying in his absence, and this confirmed the fact that I had been able to understand and to reply accurately in a language of which I was completely ignorant. (This curious experience was repeated some years later when visiting Abdu'l Baha in Paris.)

On returning the next day for another interview, I asked the Master to give me his blessing for the journey that lay ahead of me. This he did, adding casually that I should be returning to Marseilles on the following day on the same steamer from which I had so recently disembarked. I then explained to the interpreter that I had made other arrangements and that all my overland bookings had been made. He replied to the effect that if the Master said I had to return to Marseilles now, then that was what would happen.

I went back to my hotel in a state of considerable annoyance because I saw no good reason for changing my plans. During the night, a very restless one, I found myself in two minds as to what I should do. Next morning, when I went to say goodbye, and much to my own surprise, I told Abdu'l Baha that in fact I was leaving on the *Sphinx* for Marseilles later on that same day. He took this for granted and then requested me to carry out a commission for him on reaching Paris. He said that there I should meet a certain Persian student who was nearly blind, and he gave me £10 in gold to pay his fare to Alexandria. (Travelling was much cheaper in those days!) I was to tell this young man, whose name was Tammadun ul Molk, to lose no time and to present himself to his Master as soon as he arrived. I accepted this commission with very bad grace because it seemed a poor reason for upsetting all my previous plans. When I asked for the student's address in Paris I was told that this was unknown but that a way would be found for bringing me into contact with him.

On reaching Paris I went to the Persian Consulate, only to find that Tammadun ul Molk was unknown to the officials there. I then visited the student's quarter on the left bank of the Seine and spent the whole day there and elsewhere in a task that yielded no results whatever. When one's mind is fearful or depressed, no interior guidance can be expected. This I have found to be true on many occasions throughout my life. In the present instance I gave up the search and set out for the Gare du Nord, where my luggage was already deposited in readiness for the return to England. En route I crossed the Seine by the Pont Royal. Happening to look across the bridge to the opposite pavement, I saw, among a crowd of pedestrians, a young man, evidently of Eastern origin, who was using a stick to tap his way along. I dodged through the traffic and accosted him. In reply to my question, he told me he was of Persian origin. I then enquired whether by chance he knew a certain Tammadun ul Molk. In surprise he replied "C'est moi", adding that he had only arrived in Paris from Vienna that very morning. In a Vienna clinic three serious operations on his eyes had been undertaken, but the results were negative

"WE ARE ALL THE FRUITS OF ONE TREE"

and he had been told by the surgeon that his sight could not be saved.

I then gave Abdu'l Baha's message and the £10 for his ticket to Alexandria. To watch the profound joy on his face was more than sufficient reward for all my previous disappointments, including the abandonment of my European tour. Tammadun duly reached Alexandria and visited his Master at once. Those present told me later that Abdu'l Baha poured a few drops of attar of roses into a glass of water. He then gave the youth his blessing whilst anointing his eyes with the water in question. Immediately full sight was restored, and when I met Tammadun some years later he was still enjoying perfect vision.

The further sequel was both significant and instructive. I crossed to England late that night and, on reaching my office the next day, discovered that I was only just in time to avert a very serious crisis in my affairs. The change in my plans had indeed turned out to be a blessing in disguise.

On many other occasions the prophetic insight of the Baha'i leader was made clear to me. As an instance of this, I recall that when visiting him at Haifa, just after the Armistice in November 1918, I spoke of the thankfulness we all must feel that the war "to end all wars" had been fought and won. He laid his hand upon my shoulder and told me that a still greater conflagration lay ahead of humanity. "It will be largely fought out in the air, on all continents, and on the sea. Victory will lie with no one. You, my son, will still be alive to witness this tragedy and to play your part. Beyond and following many tribulations, and through the beneficence of the Supreme One, the most great peace will dawn." He always emphasised the need for unity through love to bring about

"WE ARE ALL THE FRUITS OF ONE TREE"

friendly understanding between followers of every creed, irrespective of race, colour or social status. (Extract from *The Silent Road*, Neville Spearman Ltd., London.)

CHAPTER EIGHTEEN

The Fall of Haifa and the Safeguarding of Abdu'l Baha and his Family

It must have been in the early spring of 1918 that I began to feel acute anxiety for the safety of Abdu'l Baha and his family and followers in Haifa. I came out of the line in December 1917 during the attack on Jerusalem, and being temporarily incapacitated for active service, was transferred to Intelligence, first at Cairo and later at Ludd, Jaffa and Jerusalem.

Early in March 1918 information reached me from our own espionage service that the Turkish Commander-in-Chief, whose headquarters was then between Haifa and Beirut, had stated his definite intention to take the lives of Abdu'l Baha and those around him should the Turkish Army be compelled to evacuate Haifa and retreat north.

With an advance base in and around Jaffa, we were beginning to prepare for a move towards Haifa at that time. For several reasons, including shortage of men and munitions, our advance was to be delayed well into the summer of 1918. Meanwhile, the news reaching me personally concerning Abdu'l Baha's imminent danger became more and more alarming. I tried to arouse interest in the matter among those who were responsible for

Intelligence activities (including General Clayton, Sir Wyndham Deedes, and Sir Ronald Storrs—who had recently been appointed Governor of Jerusalem), and my own chief, Major-General Sir Arthur Money (Chief Administrator of Occupied Enemy Territory). None of them knew anything about Abdu'l Baha, nor could they be made to realise the urgent need to ensure his safety.

At this time chance brought me into touch with a senior officer whose social and political connections were strong. Through his courtesy and interest I was enabled to get an urgent message through—uncensored—to the British Foreign Office in London.

Through friends associated with the Baha's cause in England, and an influential member of my own circle, an independent avenue of approach to the ruling powers was discovered and utilised.

By these means Lord Balfour, Lord Curzon, Lloyd George, Lord Milner and others in the Cabinet were warned of the critical situation at Haifa. Lord Lamington's influence proved of special help at this time. The outcome of these various activities bore good fruit, and a Cabinet despatch was sent to General Allenby instructing him to ensure the safety of Abdu'l Baha and his family and entourage so soon as the British Army captured Haifa.

This despatch passed through my hands in Cairo en route for Army H.Q. at Ludd and it was immediately passed on to be dealt with by the Staff there. No one at Headquarters had heard of Abdu'l Baha or of the Baha'i Movement, and Intelligence officials at Cairo were requested to make urgent enquiry. In due course this demand for information reached me and ultimately (when other enquiries had proved fruitless) was passed to me for action.

THE FALL OF HAIFA

As a result, General Allenby was provided with full particulars of Abdu'l Baha's life and an account of the movement of which he was the leader.

Allenby then issued orders to the General in command of the Haifa operations to the effect that immediately the town was entered, a British guard should be posted around Abdu'l Baha's house, and a further guard placed at the disposal of his family and followers. Meanwhile, we found ways of making it known within the enemy lines that stern retribution would follow any attempt to cause death or injury to Abdu'l Baha or to any of his household.

I have no doubt that this warning played an important part in averting tragedy. So soon as Haifa was captured, the instructions for posting a guard were immediately carried out, and all danger to the lives of the Master and his family was averted.

It is not possible to say for certain whether disaster would have resulted otherwise, but as the town was full of Turkish spies for some time after its capture (many of whom knew of the Turkish Commander-in-Chief's firm intention to massacre Abdu'l Baha and his family) action with this end in view might have been successfully attempted, were it not for the precautions which I have described above.

The honour and protection shown to the Baha's leader at that time were greatly appreciated by him, and this gave considerable help to British prestige in Persia and elsewhere in the Middle East. He told me this himself.

It was a wonderful experience in the midst of the chaos of war to visit the Master at his Mount Carmel home, which even at that time remained a haven of peace and refreshment.

THE FALL OF HAIFA

I well remember him, majestic yet gentle, pacing up and down the garden whilst he spoke to me about eternal realities, at a time when the whole material world was rocking on its foundations. The power of the spirit shone through his presence, giving one the feeling that a great prophet from Old Testament days had risen up in a war-stricken world, to guide and inspire all who would listen to him.

CHAPTER NINETEEN

The Master as a Seer

More than once in the presence of Abdu'l Baha I was able to glimpse the extent to which he could see the future—not merely in the working of a single life but also in the broad sweep of history.

He not only predicted the outbreak of the first world war to me in 1910 but, in fact, indicated the whole course of the twentieth century. In a letter which I sent from Egypt at that time to a friend in Scotland I wrote as follows:

"The Master states definitely that regeneration and social and moral progress will take place in Persia and that this country will ultimately become a free and constitutionally governed nation of considerable prestige. He told me that Britain had done much of real value and importance for the welfare of India and Egypt, but he anticipated nevertheless a world-wide upheaval, to be preceded by a European war, probably within the next five years. This, he said, nothing can avert.

"It would appear that the seeds for this grave conflict have already been sown in the Balkans. It is evident that we are to expect in our own lifetime a lengthy period of wars and revolutions embodying what could be interpreted as becoming the Armageddon prophesied to take place at the end of this present age or dispensation.

"Whilst the Master seems entirely confident that the

coming of 'The Most Great Peace', accompanied by worldwide brotherhood, is destined to come into being following this long period of Armageddon, the date of such a consummation cannot be foretold.

"It was during this visit that the Master gave me his blessing and allowed me to understand that the time would come when I should be destined to play a particular role in human affairs, without, however, specifying in detail the direction in which my mission would lie . . ."

While the 1914-18 war was still being fought Abdu'l Baha was able on more than one occasion to reassure his followers about the outcome of local events.

During the British advance from the south in 1918, field batteries had been placed in position immediately to the south east of Mount Carmel, the intention being to shell Haifa at long range over the Mount itself. Some of the Baha'is living on the Mount becoming agitated, went to Abdu'l Baha's home to express their alarm. According to an eye witness of this scene (from whom I obtained the story when I reached Haifa), Abdu'l Baha calmed all fears and called his followers to prayer. Then he assured them that all would be well, and that no British shells would cause death or damage to Haifa itself or to those living there. As a matter of historical fact, it turned out that the range of the field batteries in question proved inaccurate, the shells passing harmlessly over the town and falling into the Bay of Akka beyond.

Another incident of those times is worthy of record, although I am not able to vouch for its accuracy at first hand. I was told by a reliable witness that before the fall of Haifa, Abdu'l Baha was discussing the British campaign with those around him. He then predicted that, contrary to the general expectation, the taking of Haifa and the walled town of Akka would be achieved almost without bloodshed. This prediction was borne out by events. He also stated that the Turks would surrender the fortress town of Akka (supposed to be impregnable) to two unarmed British soldiers. The facts so far as I was able to gather turned out to be as follows:

After our entry into Haifa, the front line was pushed forward halfway across the Bay of Akka, and outposts were placed in position on the sands of the Bay some five miles from Akka itself. Akka was believed to be filled with Turkish troops at this time.

Very early next morning two British Army Service men, who had lost their bearings in the night, found themselves at the gates of Akka, believing erroneously that the town was already in British hands. However, the Turkish rearguard troops had been secretly evacuated some hours earlier, and the Mayor of the town, seeing British soldiers outside the gates, came down and presented them with the keys of the town in token of surrender!

It was at about this time that the Master and I talked over the steps then being taken to prepare a home for the whole Jewish people in Palestine. Currently I was deeply concerned about the probable fate of long existing Christian settlements in Palestine.

This concern was shared by the Master but he never allowed himself to become involved in political issues. The comment he made at the time, however, struck me with great force, and it is a tragedy that his words went unheeded both then and since. This is what he said: "The world of humanity owes to the Jews a homestead of their own. Let those who are responsible for kindling the flame in this new hearth see to it that the heat warms and does not scorch both friends and neighbours alike." If such wisdom had been heeded we could have averted the wars and persecutions that have proved so tragic a feature of the birth and stormy history of the State of Israel.

CHAPTER TWENTY

The Prison House of St. Jean D'Acre

(extract from a letter written in November 1918)

I have just visited the prison house of Baha'u'llah and spent some time in the company of Abdu'l Baha and his family.

How often have I pictured myself in these surroundings. I have longed to be here ever since those distant days in 1908 when I first heard of the Baha'is and their Master.

A long stone stairway leads up to the living rooms in this prison house where Baha'u'llah spent the last portion of his life and where his son was confined until his release in 1908. The stairway is worn thin by the feet of the countless pilgrims who have passed up and down for so many years.

The Master was standing at the top waiting to greet me, with that sweet smile and cheery welcome for which he is famous. For the seventy-four years of his life Abdu'l Baha has lived in the midst of tragedy and hardship, yet nothing affects his cheery optimism, spiritual insight and keen sense of humour. He was looking a little older than when I saw him seven years ago but certainly more vigorous than when in England after his exhausting American tour.

His voice is as strong as ever, his eyes clear, his step

THE PRISON HOUSE OF ST. JEAN D'ACRE

virile; his hair and beard are (if possible) more silvery white than before. He is delighted to welcome the change of regime, but I could detect a tragic note, for, if the British occupation had happened earlier he would still have felt young enough to travel throughout the Near and Middle East spreading his father's message. Baha'i proselytising has never been allowed (by A.B.) in the Turkish Empire and now the Master is too old to stir far from his home on Mount Carmel. He still spends a few weeks now and again in the Akka prison house, that has recently become his property.

After lunch he drove me out to the garden tomb of Baha'u'llah about two miles from the city. His loving reverence for his father is unbounded. He approached the tomb in complete silence, praying with bowed head, a wonderfully venerable figure in his white turban and flowing robe. On reaching the portal to the Tomb itself, the Master prostrated himself at full length and kissed the steps leading to the inner chamber. There was a majestic humility about the action defying description. I, with my Anglo-Saxon stolidity, could not find courage enough to follow his example in front of the Persian believers standing by.

We then took tea in the garden and A.B. told many stories about Baha'u'llah—his superhuman endurance, his courage and his noble teaching. When we returned to Akka, the Persian colony, consisting of perhaps thirty-five persons, had assembled and we sat round the room drinking tea, whilst A.B. described his visit to my home in Clifton and spoke of the people he had met there. I then left to pay my respects to Major Beaumont, the Military Governor, curious to discover what he knew of, and felt about the greatest religious personage in Asia today.

The Governor was much occupied with a demonstration he was arranging for the morrow in celebration of world peace. A band was coming, the notables of Akka were to process round the town, and the Governor would then acknowledge cheers and make a speech from the balcony of the Town Hall. A notable occasion for Akka and its people freed after so many hundreds of years from the harsh Turkish yoke!

I enquired whether Abdu'l Baha had been invited to the function. "Do you mean Abbas Effendi? Well, no, I don't think we've asked him. Perhaps he should have an invitation!"

The man who has worked night and day for over fifty years to propagate the ideals of world peace and brotherhood, whose devoted followers number several million, whose cause is doing so much to lessen religious discord in the East—this man had not even received an invitation to take part in the peace celebrations of his native town! This is because (as it turned out) his name did not appear on the list of local notables prepared by the municipal authorities for the guidance of the Governor!

"A prophet in his own country without honour" with a vengeance! I expressed mild surprise (the shock had driven indignation from me) and an invitation was duly despatched. I then returned to the prison-house and spent the evening with the Master, supping with him and answering his questions about the new Palestine administration. I slept in the room next to A.B.'s (which had been his father's before him).

These were simple attics with stone floors and practically

no furniture. A.B. still gives away all possessions and lives the life of poverty himself. Before breakfast the house was filled with believers who had come to receive the morning blessing. I had brought A.B. letters from many parts of the world, and he spent the morning in dictating replies for me to take away.

At lunch we had another heart-to-heart talk during which the Master referred to the truth that to human sense a life of service and integrity should not end in sorrow and distress, but it should merge naturally into to a wider world with joy and thanksgiving. I think he was referring, to a large extent, to those who, in doing their duty in wars and revolutions, had seemingly left earth life before their allotted span.

He then spoke of the oneness of Life, the ultimate victory over "death", that last enemy, which will be defeated when mankind conquers sin, selfishness and fear, and learns to reflect the light and love of the one Creator of us all.

The point of particular interest in connection with this experience was this. I understand and speak no Persian, and only a little Arabic. The Master spoke in Persian and no interpreter was present. It was only later on, when we were joined by others (one of whom spoke English) that I realised with amazement that I had understood all that he had been saying, and that it had seemed quite natural to have done so.

Soon after lunch came the leave taking and the Master's blessing. He sent greetings by me to all his friends in Egypt, Europe, England and America. As I drove off on my return to Haifa, I caught a parting glimpse of him, staff in hand, wending his way through terrible slums on his way to attend the local peace celebrations. Seen in his own eastern surroundings, he stands out a majestic figure, simple, wise beyond words, inspired—a fitting leader of a movement destined to influence the religious future of the world!

And here I am again on Mount Carmel writing this letter with the moonlit sea before me. I have paid my visit to the Governor of Haifa and tomorrow am free to explore the Mount, to visit the Tomb of the Bab. A.B. himself will not return here for another week. He is helping to solve religious problems that have arisen in the Akka area as the result of the British occupation.

Though by no means a fanatic, I am bound to say that my visit to these places, sacred to Baha'u'llah and his son, have deepened my conviction that the Baha'i movement has an important part to play in the religious regeneration of the world, and especially the Eastern world.

In Abdu'l Baha's presence, one became aware—dimly perhaps, but surely—of that serene security which comes from an understanding that One Mind embraces the whole universe, and that we are all brothers within this universe and are eternally at one with the Mind which controls it. Such a truth, familiar as it is to all religions, seems to be a far cry from our daily experience, but this practice of the Master to align *all* experience to a universal concept remains with me as the keynote to his life and teaching. I suppose it is inevitable that we should descend from the heights of such a concept, and slip back into the confines of sects, dogmas and conflicting organisations. As a result, the universal note is lost, and the realisation of the Fatherhood of God and the Brotherhood of all men becomes dim and mythical.

It is easier to become nearer to this truth in *silence* rather than in speech. In the deeps of silence, we are all one, and it is through interior stillness that knowledge of our oneness with the Creator reaches us. It has been truly said that the voice of silence carries infinitely farther than the loudest cry. Such a union as this can never be ours except in silence, and through stillness and deep prayer and meditation we can begin to comprehend the meaning of Infinity and of that one Mind in which we all live and move and have our being.

On looking back after so many years have passed, to those times when I was privileged to know Abdu'l Baha in bodily form, perhaps the most unfading memory left can be summed up by these two words: *Unity and Silence*: and it is not a far cry, in reality, to translate these two words into Love and Wisdom—Unity the outcome of Love and Wisdom the outcome of Silence.

Footnote: Further information about the Baha'i Teaching can be obtained from the Baha'i Trust, 27 Rutland Gate, London, S.W.7.

CHAPTER TWENTY-ONE

Vision on the Mount
(on the evening of 18th of November 1918)

I was staying at the German Hospice on Mount Scopus overlooking the Mount of Olives. The moon was nearly full; a silvery grey mist crept up from the Jordan Valley, hiding the Mountains of Moab and the Dead Sea. The air seemed full of mystery. I retired early and sat out on my balcony. For a time my mind was full of the problems up for discussion that day; the political future of Damascus; the attitude of Lebanese Druses; the ever-present Jewish problems in Palestine; the situation at Beirut, and so on indefinitely. Soon all these thoughts vanished and then, as I gazed out upon the silver sea that surrounded the Mount, I saw Jesus walking on the "waves". When is vision actual? Who can tell? It was the Master of two thousand years ago; his eyes were full of light and he seemed to be watching, prophetically, the growth and spread of the Illumination he had come into the world to radiate . . . he seemed sad, yet full of hope and even fiery optimism; the first page of the Christian era was opening. And then the silvery mist rose around him and I saw no more, but later, as I was going to bed, Jesus stood upon the Mount and wept. It was the same figure, yet not the same, for two thousand years had nearly passed away and the Book of the Christian Era was open in his hands, *open towards the last page*. I cannot describe the effect upon me of this vision of divine tragedy. The pages of the Book seemed to turn before my eyes, back, back through the centuries. And many pages were so black and the Christ spirit seemed to become dim as the pages turned, backward, forward, until again was shown the terrible writing on the last pages. When it seemed as if all were over and that a pit of darkness yawned before his feet, suddenly a new divine radiance descended around him and he was caught up in a cloud of flame that seemed to bathe the whole world in the glorious hues of sunrise. I wonder what it all meant; Is the new Era on its way? Are there many Saviours coming to our rescue, or only One?

EPILOGUE

God is Love?

Many good and thoughtful Christians earnestly desire to believe in a God of infinite love, despite the apparent fact that this all powerful Being appears to allow and to tolerate pain, cruelty and injustice in human affairs. Theology does not appear to have ever equipped itself to explain this age-old conundrum, or to discover the key to its solution.

"God" is depicted by so many of our teachers as a kind of super human "man" who doles out His blessings to the minority He favours, and subjects the rest of us to pain, sorrow and despair.

Finite understanding is incapable of equating this seeming paradox, yet I believe that clues *are* available.

Our quest for enlightenment is unlikely to make progress so long as we regard the creative Source of the myriads of universes which are known to exist, as if He were a person, a kind of gigantic individual, capable of being everywhere at the same time. Even to our finite understanding such a conception makes no sense. On the other hand, if we try to define the supreme Creator as a Principle, the principle underlying all Life, Love and Wisdom, there is the danger that we may think of "God" in terms of a machine rather than as a supreme, eternal and omnipresent Mind. Whilst we shrink from the idea of offering our love and our prayers to a machine, we can perhaps grasp the conception of a universal Intelligence, permeating the whole of Creation and through whom the principles of Life, Love and Wisdom manifest unceasingly.

Whilst this Intelligence can be conceived as a Father figure, it is wise to remember that there is no manifestation of life and mind which does not contain within itself the Divine attributes of the Godhead.

Should you agree with me so far, then you will probably accept the thesis that God the supreme Principle has provided Man with a certain measure of free will, and access at all times to the ability to receive and utilise His love to the full extent of our various capabilities and our Will to God.

This Love, under human conditions, can only operate through us as its channel of activity. This is my firm belief. Used rightly it can ultimately solve all our human problems: destroy famine and wars, disease, injustice, sorrow, pain and cruelty in every form. But only through us as its medium of manifestation.

"God" does not pour out His beneficence like rain from the skies, intermittently, externally and haphazardly. This Beneficence can only operate THROUGH US, both as individuals and communities. There is enough of it and to spare to solve all our problems, if we use the gift of free will rightly.

Surely it stands to reason that to the extent that the creative Principle grants a measure of free will to His "children" to the same extent does He limit the exercise of His Omnipotence in their affairs? (An instance of transfer of power from the Creator to the created.) To regain absolute Omnipotence it would be necessary for God to deprive man of his free will altogether. No doubt this could happen should we abuse the power we possess beyond a prescribed and fore-determined limit of divine toleration. (A return to the stage of robots?)

It is not God who tolerates and condones this world's woes but we ourselves, because we do not use the ever-flowing bounty of Love in our own lives and actions.

In this respect, God cannot operate behind our backs or against the free will which is our heritage.

For the reasons given above it is surely true to believe that God cannot intervene over our heads and put the world right INDEPENDENTLY of our willing co-operation?

To take concrete examples.

There is ample air, light and water FREELY available to us (subject to the adequate redistribution of the latter) to enable man to convert all this planet's desert areas into fruitful granaries. Even as matters stand today, given proper and rapid distribution, there are enough foodstuffs available to banish famine everywhere. And in regard to the population explosion, we have the power and the means to bring this dangerous situation under control. Indeed, if we do not do so, Nature will take a hand and bring about decimation in her own, and in fact, seemingly cruel way, mainly through the propagation of killing diseases on a world-wide scale.

In order to halt the crumbling of the moral standards of our modern civilisation, a revision of priorities, long overdue, is URGENT. It is estimated, for instance, that less than half the money and energy spent on moon and spatial probes would have proved sufficient to rid our planet of famine altogether. The immense expenditure to date on the stockpiling of nuclear weapons (many of them already out of date), would have proved sufficient, if used constructively, WITH SPIRITUAL INTENT, to have transformed the world for the better, beyond our most optimistic dreams. Here are instances where the choice has been ours to make.

Omnipotence? Yes, but (so far as our planet is concerned) THROUGH the agency of human channels, aided by those unseen Christ inspired Beings and Energies who are always ready to hear and to respond to our call. Man himself contains within himself the seeds of omnipotence and salvation. To think otherwise is to refuse our birthright and to negative its very existence.

The fundamental question that remains and to which we humans can give no satisfying answer is this: How can a "God", the Creator of perfection, visualise Life forms which can become subject to imperfection?

Inevitably we are now in the regions of surmise. At some point in the very distant past it would seem that a hitch took place in the orderly advance of the evolutionary process. As a result, and probably for lengthy periods, devolution stepped in. The seeds of evolution appear to have been stamped underground, but their germinating power, although stagnant during this very lengthy period, has never become sterile.

Human reasoning at its present stage of comprehension, is bound to postulate the thesis that what we call the Fall of Man into matter did actually take place. We cannot prove this belief and it is useless to try to do so. What I for one DO believe, however, is that we are now at a point in human history where the devolutionary process is being gradually halted, and is about to be turned in a progressive direction once more.

EPILOGUE

Let us pray that this is so, and work for it . . .

YES, GOD IS LOVE. And we can prove it—The more love we reflect and share with one another, the greater will be the supply available to us: a supply that is infinite, boundless, never failing and eternal.

When the truth of this realisation is recognised and utilised we shall be on the first lap of the road leading to the arrival of "Heaven on Earth".

May God speed the day!

Since *The Silent Road* was written, it has been drawn to my attention that certain Baha'i Institutions were established by Baha'u'llah in Persia during His lifetime, and that the Master had prepared an outline of the world administrative order set forth in His written Testament. This is not incompatible with what Abdu'l Baha conveyed to me, as Baha'is regard their Faith as the perennial Religion of God in its latest form. The Faith had then reached the stage similar to early Christianity, when the distinction between Jewish and Christian organisation and adherents was not yet apparent. The passing of Abdu'l Baha ended the "Heroic Age", and in this subsequent "Formative Age", the distinction between those who adhere to this Faith and those who do not, again becomes apparent, as those institutions envisaged by Baha'u'llah and elaborated by the Master are established, Baha'is believe that the Local and National Assemblies, and the Universal House of Justice now formed, is the divinely appointed framework for building World Unity and peace, prophesied by Jesus, The Christ, when He said, "and there shall be One Fold and One Shepherd".

Paperbacks also available from White Crow Books

Elsa Barker—*Letters from a Living Dead Man*
ISBN 978-1-907355-83-7

Elsa Barker—*War Letters from the Living Dead Man*
ISBN 978-1-907355-85-1

Elsa Barker—*Last Letters from the Living Dead Man*
ISBN 978-1-907355-87-5

Richard Maurice Bucke—*Cosmic Consciousness*
ISBN 978-1-907355-10-3

Stafford Betty—*The Imprisoned Splendor*
ISBN 978-1-907661-98-3

Stafford Betty—*Heaven and Hell Unveiled: Updates from the World of Spirit.*
ISBN 978-1-910121-30-6

Ineke Koedam—*In the Light of Death: Experiences on the threshold between life and death*
ISBN 978-1-910121-48-1

Arthur Conan Doyle with Simon Parke—*Conversations with Arthur Conan Doyle*
ISBN 978-1-907355-80-6

Meister Eckhart with Simon Parke—*Conversations with Meister Eckhart*
ISBN 978-1-907355-18-9

D. D. Home—*Incidents in my Life Part 1*
ISBN 978-1-907355-15-8

Mme. Dunglas Home; edited, with an Introduction, by Sir Arthur Conan Doyle—*D. D. Home: His Life and Mission*
ISBN 978-1-907355-16-5

Edward C. Randall—*Frontiers of the Afterlife*
ISBN 978-1-907355-30-1

Rebecca Ruter Springer—*Intra Muros: My Dream of Heaven*
ISBN 978-1-907355-11-0

Leo Tolstoy, edited by Simon Parke—*Forbidden Words*
ISBN 978-1-907355-00-4

Erlendur Haraldsson and Loftur Gissurarson—*Indridi Indridason: The Icelandic Physical Medium*
ISBN 978-1-910121-50-4

Goerge E. Moss—*Earth's Cosmic Ascendancy: Spirit and Extraterrestrials Guide us through Times of Change*
ISBN 978-1-910121-28-3

Steven T. Parsons and Callum E. Cooper—*Paracoustics: Sound & the Paranormal*
ISBN 978-1-910121-32-0

L. C. Danby—*The Certainty of Eternity: The Story of Australia's Greatest Medium*
ISBN 978-1-910121-34-4

Madelaine Lawrence —*The Death View Revolution: A Guide to Transpersonal Experiences Surrounding Death*
ISBN 978-1-910121-37-5

Zofia Weaver—*Other Realities?: The enigma of Franek Kluski's mediumship*
ISBN 978-1-910121-39-9

Roy L. Hill—*Psychology and the Near-Death Experience: Searching for God*
ISBN 978-1-910121-42-9

Tricia. J. Robertson —*"Things You Can do When You're Dead!: True Accounts of After Death Communication"*
ISBN 978-1-908733-60-3

Tricia. J. Robertson —*More Things you Can do When You're Dead: What Can You Truly Believe?*
ISBN 978-1-910121-44-3

Jody Long—*God's Fingerprints: Impressions of Near-Death Experiences*
ISBN 978-1-910121-05-4

Leo Tolstoy with Simon Parke—*Conversations with Tolstoy*
ISBN 978-1-907355-25-7

Howard Williams with an Introduction by Leo Tolstoy—*The Ethics of Diet: An Anthology of Vegetarian Thought*
ISBN 978-1-907355-21-9

Vincent Van Gogh with Simon Parke—*Conversations with Van Gogh*
ISBN 978-1-907355-95-0

Wolfgang Amadeus Mozart with Simon Parke—*Conversations with Mozart*
ISBN 978-1-907661-38-9

Jesus of Nazareth with Simon Parke—*Conversations with Jesus of Nazareth*
ISBN 978-1-907661-41-9

Thomas à Kempis with Simon Parke—*The Imitation of Christ*
ISBN 978-1-907661-58-7

Julian of Norwich with Simon Parke—*Revelations of Divine Love*
ISBN 978-1-907661-88-4

Allan Kardec—*The Spirits Book*
ISBN 978-1-907355-98-1

Allan Kardec—*The Book on Mediums*
ISBN 978-1-907661-75-4

Emanuel Swedenborg—*Heaven and Hell*
ISBN 978-1-907661-55-6

P.D. Ouspensky—*Tertium Organum: The Third Canon of Thought*
ISBN 978-1-907661-47-1

Dwight Goddard—*A Buddhist Bible*
ISBN 978-1-907661-44-0

Michael Tymn—*The Afterlife Revealed*
ISBN 978-1-970661-90-7

Michael Tymn—*Transcending the Titanic: Beyond Death's Door*
ISBN 978-1-908733-02-3

Guy L. Playfair—*If This Be Magic*
ISBN 978-1-907661-84-6

Guy L. Playfair—*The Flying Cow*
ISBN 978-1-907661-94-5

Guy L. Playfair —*This House is Haunted: The True Story of the Enfield Poltergeist*
ISBN 978-1-907661-78-5

Carl Wickland, M.D.—*Thirty Years Among the Dead*
ISBN 978-1-907661-72-3

John E. Mack—*Passport to the Cosmos*
ISBN 978-1-907661-81-5

Peter & Elizabeth Fenwick—*The Truth in the Light*
ISBN 978-1-908733-08-5

Erlendur Haraldsson— *Modern Miracles*
ISBN 978-1-908733-25-2

Erlendur Haraldsson— *At the Hour of Death*
ISBN 978-1-908733-27-6

Erlendur Haraldsson—*The Departed Among the Living*
ISBN 978-1-908733-29-0

Brian Inglis—*Science and Parascience*
ISBN 978-1-908733-18-4

Brian Inglis—*Natural and Supernatural: A History of the Paranormal*
ISBN 978-1-908733-20-7

Ernest Holmes—*The Science of Mind*
ISBN 978-1-908733-10-8

Victor & Wendy Zammit —*A Lawyer Presents the Evidence For the Afterlife*
ISBN 978-1-908733-22-1

Casper S. Yost—*Patience Worth: A Psychic Mystery*
ISBN 978-1-908733-06-1

William Usborne Moore—*Glimpses of the Next State*
ISBN 978-1-907661-01-3

William Usborne Moore—*The Voices*
ISBN 978-1-908733-04-7

John W. White—*The Highest State of Consciousness*
ISBN 978-1-908733-31-3

Lord Dowding—*Many Mansions*
ISBN 978-1-910121-07-8

Paul Pearsall, Ph.D. —*Super Joy*
ISBN 978-1-908733-16-0

All titles available as eBooks, and selected titles available in Hardback and Audiobook formats from www.whitecrowbooks.com

www.ingramcontent.com/pod-product-compliance
Lightning Source LLC
LaVergne TN
LVHW090115080426
835507LV00040B/894